MznLnx

Missing Links Exam Preps

Exam Prep for

Valuation: Measuring and Managing the Value of Companies

Koller, Goedhart, & Wessels, 4th Edition

The MznLnx Exam Prep is your link from the texbook and lecture to your exams.
The MznLnx Exam Preps are unauthorized and comprehensive reviews of your textbooks.

All material provided by MznLnx and Rico Publications (c) 2010
Textbook publishers and textbook authors do not particpate in or contribute to these reviews.

MznLnx

Rico Publications

Exam Prep for Valuation: Measuring and Managing the Value of Companies
4th Edition
Koller, Goedhart, & Wessels

Publisher: Raymond Houge
Assistant Editor: Michael Rouger
Text and Cover Designer: Lisa Buckner
Marketing Manager: Sara Swagger
Project Manager, Editorial Production: Jerry Emerson
Art Director: Vernon Lowerui

Product Manager: Dave Mason
Editorial Asitant: Rachel Guzmanji
Pedagogy: Debra Long
Cover Image: Jim Reed/Getty Images
Text and Cover Printer: City Printing, Inc.
Compositor: Media Mix, Inc.

(c) 2010 Rico Publications
ALL RIGHTS RESERVED. No part of this work covered by the copyright may be reproduced or used in any form or by an means--graphic, electronic, or mechanical, including photocopying, recording, taping, Web distribution, information storage, and retrieval systems, or in any other manner--without the written permission of the publisher.

Printed in the United States
ISBN:

For more information about our products, contact us at:
Dave.Mason@RicoPublications.com

For permission to use material from this text or product, submit a request online to:
Dave.Mason@RicoPublications.com

Contents

CHAPTER 1
Why Maximize Value? 1

CHAPTER 2
The Value Manager 4

CHAPTER 3
Fundamental Principles of Value Creation 6

CHAPTER 4
Do Fundamentals Really Drive the Stock Market? 10

CHAPTER 5
Frameworks for Valuation 15

CHAPTER 6
Thinking about Return on Invested Capital and Growth 23

CHAPTER 7
Analyzing Historical Performance 26

CHAPTER 8
Forecasting Performance 40

CHAPTER 9
Estimating Continuing Value 48

CHAPTER 10
Estimating the Cost of Capital 51

CHAPTER 11
Calculating and Interpreting Results 59

CHAPTER 12
Using Multiples for Valuation 64

CHAPTER 13
Performance Measurement 67

CHAPTER 14
Performance Management 69

CHAPTER 15
Creating Value through Mergers and Acquisitions 71

CHAPTER 16
Creating Value through Divestitures 74

CHAPTER 17
Capital Structure 75

CHAPTER 18
Investor Communications 82

CHAPTER 19
Valuing Multibusiness Companies 85

CHAPTER 20
Valuing Flexibility 88

Contents (Cont.)

CHAPTER 21
   Cross-Border Valuation — 91

CHAPTER 22
   Valuation in Emerging Markets — 100

CHAPTER 23
   Valuing High-Growth Companies — 107

CHAPTER 24
   Valuing Cyclical Companies — 109

CHAPTER 25
   Valuing Financial Institutions — 110

ANSWER KEY — 117

TO THE STUDENT

COMPREHENSIVE

The *MznLnx* Exam Prep series is designed to help you pass your exams. Editors at MznLnx review your textbooks and then prepare these practice exams to help you master the textbook material. Unlike study guides, workbooks, and practice tests provided by the texbook publisher and textbook authors, *MznLnx* gives you **all** of the material in each chapter in exam form, not just samples, so you can be sure to nail your exam.

MECHANICAL

The MznLnx Exam Prep series creates exams that will help you learn the subject matter as well as test you on your understanding. Each question is designed to help you master the concept. Just working through the exams, you gain an understanding of the subject--its a simple mechanical process that produces success.

INTEGRATED STUDY GUIDE AND REVIEW

MznLnx is not just a set of exams designed to test you, its also a comprehensive review of the subject content. Each exam question is also a review of the concept, making sure that you will get the answer correct without having to go to other sources of material. You learn as you go! Its the easiest way to pass an exam.

HUMOR

Studying can be tedious and dry. MznLnx's instructional design includes moderate humor within the exam questions on occassion, to break the tedium and revitalize the brain

Chapter 1. Why Maximize Value?

1. A _____ is the direction in which a financial market is moving. _____s can be classified as primary trends, secondary trends (short-term), and secular trends (long-term.) This principle incorporates the idea that market cycles occur with regularity and persistence.
   a. 7-Eleven
   b. 4-4-5 Calendar
   c. Market trend
   d. 529 plan

2. A _____ is a private or public market for the trading of company stock and derivatives of company stock at an agreed price; these are securities listed on a stock exchange as well as those only traded privately.

   The size of the world _____ is estimated at about $36.6 trillion US at the beginning of October 2008 . The world derivatives market has been estimated at about $480 trillion face or nominal value, 12 times the size of the entire world economy.

   a. Stock market
   b. Adolph Coors
   c. Anton Gelonkin
   d. Andrew Tobias

3. In economic models, the _____ time frame assumes no fixed factors of production. Firms can enter or leave the marketplace, and the cost (and availability) of land, labor, raw materials, and capital goods can be assumed to vary. In contrast, in the short-run time frame, certain factors are assumed to be fixed, because there is not sufficient time for them to change.
   a. 4-4-5 Calendar
   b. Long-run
   c. Short-run
   d. 529 plan

4. In finance, _____ refers to the value of a security which is intrinsic to or contained in the security itself. It is also frequently called fundamental value. It is ordinarily calculated by summing the future income generated by the asset, and discounting it to the present value.
   a. Alpha
   b. Accretion
   c. Amortization
   d. Intrinsic value

5. _____ is an economic concept with commonplace familiarity. It is the price that a good or service is offered at, or will fetch, in the marketplace. It is of interest mainly in the study of microeconomics.
   a. Central Securities Depository
   b. Delta hedging
   c. Convertible arbitrage
   d. Market price

6. In probability theory and statistics, a _____ is described as the number separating the higher half of a sample, a population, or a probability distribution from the lower half. The _____ of a finite list of numbers can be found by arranging all the observations from lowest value to highest value and picking the middle one. If there is an even number of observations, the _____ is not unique, so one often takes the mean of the two middle values.
   a. Geometric mean
   b. Standard deviation
   c. Variance
   d. Median

7. The institution most often referenced by the word '_____' is a public or publicly traded _____, the shares of which are traded on a public stock exchange (e.g., the New York Stock Exchange or Nasdaq in the United States) where shares of stock of _____s are bought and sold by and to the general public. Most of the largest businesses in the world are publicly traded _____s. However, the majority of _____s are said to be closely held, privately held or close _____s, meaning that no ready market exists for the trading of shares.

Chapter 1. Why Maximize Value?

a. Federal Home Loan Mortgage Corporation
b. Depository Trust Company
c. Protect
d. Corporation

8. In business and finance, a _____ (also referred to as equity _____) of stock means a _____ of ownership in a corporation (company.) In the plural, stocks is often used as a synonym for _____s especially in the United States, but it is less commonly used that way outside of North America.

In the United Kingdom, South Africa, and Australia, stock can also refer to completely different financial instruments such as government bonds or, less commonly, to all kinds of marketable securities.

a. Share
b. Procter ' Gamble
c. Bucket shop
d. Margin

9. The _____ is an American stock exchange. It is the largest electronic screen-based equity securities trading market in the United States. With approximately 3,200 companies, it has more trading volume per day than any other stock exchange in the world.

a. 529 plan
b. 7-Eleven
c. 4-4-5 Calendar
d. NASDAQ

10. In finance, _____ is the process of estimating the potential market value of a financial asset or liability. they can be done on assets (for example, investments in marketable securities such as stocks, options, business enterprises, or intangible assets such as patents and trademarks) or on liabilities (e.g., Bonds issued by a company.) _____s are required in many contexts including investment analysis, capital budgeting, merger and acquisition transactions, financial reporting, taxable events to determine the proper tax liability, and in litigation.

a. Procter ' Gamble
b. Share
c. Valuation
d. Margin

11. In economics and business, a _____ is the effect that one user of a good or service has on the value of that product to other users.

The classic example is the telephone. The more people own telephones, the more valuable the telephone is to each owner.

a. 4-4-5 Calendar
b. Network effect
c. 529 plan
d. 7-Eleven

12. _____ is the set of processes, customs, policies, laws and institutions affecting the way a corporation is directed, administered or controlled. _____ also includes the relationships among the many stakeholders involved and the goals for which the corporation is governed. The principal stakeholders are the shareholders, management and the board of directors.

a. Corporate governance
b. Foreign Corrupt Practices Act
c. Patent
d. Due diligence

13. The phrase _____ according to the Organization for Economic Co-operation and Development, refers to 'creative work undertaken on a systematic basis in order to increase the stock of knowledge, including knowledge of (hu)man, culture and society, and the use of this stock of knowledge to devise new applications'.

New product design and development is more than often a crucial factor in the survival of a company. In an industry that is fast changing, firms must continually revise their design and range of products. This is necessary due to continuous technology change and development as well as other competitors and the changing preference of customers.

a. 4-4-5 Calendar
c. 7-Eleven
b. Research and development
d. 529 plan

Chapter 2. The Value Manager

1. In finance, _____ is the process of estimating the potential market value of a financial asset or liability. they can be done on assets (for example, investments in marketable securities such as stocks, options, business enterprises, or intangible assets such as patents and trademarks) or on liabilities (e.g., Bonds issued by a company.) _____s are required in many contexts including investment analysis, capital budgeting, merger and acquisition transactions, financial reporting, taxable events to determine the proper tax liability, and in litigation.

   a. Procter ' Gamble
   b. Share
   c. Margin
   d. Valuation

2. _____ is the process whereby an organization establishes the parameters within which programs, investments, and acquisitions are reaching the desired results. Performance Reference Model of the Federal Enterprise Architecture, 2005.

   This process of measuring performance ofter requires the use of statistical evidence to determine progress toward specific defined organizational objectives.

   There are many types of measurements.

   a. Decentralization
   b. Cash cow
   c. Corporate Transparency
   d. Performance measurement

3. _____ represents the total cash investment that shareholders and debtholders have made in a company. There are two different but completely equivalent methods for calculating _____. The operating approach is calculated as:

   _____ = Operating Net Working Capital + Net PP'E + Capitalized Operating Leases + Other Operating Assets + Operating Intangibles - Other Operating Liabilities - Cumulative Adjustment for Amortization of R'D

   Equivalently, the financing approach is calculated as:

   In symbols:

   $$K = D + E - M$$

   _____ is used in several important measurements of financial performance, including return on _____, economic value added, and free cash flow.

   a. Operating leverage
   b. Inventory turnover
   c. Information ratio
   d. Invested capital

4. _____ is a financial measure that quantifies how well a company generates cash flow relative to the capital it has invested in its business. It is defined as Net operating profit less adjusted taxes divided by Invested Capital and is usually expressed as a percentage. In this calculation, capital invested includes all monetary capital invested: long-term debt, common and preferred shares.

   a. Return on invested capital
   b. Sharpe ratio
   c. Cash conversion cycle
   d. Debt service coverage ratio

Chapter 2. The Value Manager

5. _____ is pay or salary, typically monetary payment for services rendered, as in an employment. Usage is considered formal.

_____ can include:

- Commission
- Compensation methods (in online advertising and internet marketing)
- Compensation
    - Executive compensation
    - Deferred compensation
- Employee stock option
- Fringe benefit
- Salary
- Wage

a. 529 plan
b. Remuneration
c. 7-Eleven
d. 4-4-5 Calendar

6. An _____ is a contract written by a seller that conveys to the buyer the right -- but not the obligation -- to buy (in the case of a call _____) or to sell (in the case of a put _____) a particular asset, such as a piece of property such as, among others, a futures contract. In return for granting the _____, the seller collects a payment (the premium) from the buyer.

For example, buying a call _____ provides the right to buy a specified quantity of a security at a set strike price at some time on or before expiration, while buying a put _____ provides the right to sell.

a. Annuity
b. Amortization
c. AT'T Mobility LLC
d. Option

Chapter 3. Fundamental Principles of Value Creation

1. _____ represents the total cash investment that shareholders and debtholders have made in a company. There are two different but completely equivalent methods for calculating _____. The operating approach is calculated as:

_____ = Operating Net Working Capital + Net PP'E + Capitalized Operating Leases + Other Operating Assets + Operating Intangibles - Other Operating Liabilities - Cumulative Adjustment for Amortization of R'D

Equivalently, the financing approach is calculated as:

In symbols:

$$K = D + E - M$$

_____ is used in several important measurements of financial performance, including return on _____, economic value added, and free cash flow.

a. Information ratio
b. Inventory turnover
c. Invested capital
d. Operating leverage

2. _____ is a financial measure that quantifies how well a company generates cash flow relative to the capital it has invested in its business. It is defined as Net operating profit less adjusted taxes divided by Invested Capital and is usually expressed as a percentage. In this calculation, capital invested includes all monetary capital invested: long-term debt, common and preferred shares.
a. Sharpe ratio
b. Debt service coverage ratio
c. Cash conversion cycle
d. Return on invested capital

3. _____ is a finance term describing a firm's non-Equity cash flows. Theoretically, adding the discounted _____ to the discounted Flows to equity (also known as Equity Cash Flows) will give the firm's Enterprise Value. The Enterprise value is the valuation obtained by calculating the Discounted Cash Flow.
a. Par value
b. Foreign exchange hedge
c. Consignment stock
d. Debt cash flow

4. Pure _____ is the increase in wealth that an investor has from making an investment, taking into consideration all costs associated with that investment including the opportunity cost of capital.

A key difficulty in measuring profit is in defining costs. Pure economic monetary profits can be zero or negative even in competitive equilibrium when accounted monetized costs exceed monetized price.

a. Economic profit
b. AAB
c. Operating profit
d. A Random Walk Down Wall Street

5. _____ is the difference between price and the costs of bringing to market whatever it is that is accounted as an enterprise (whether by harvest, extraction, manufacture, or purchase) in terms of the component costs of delivered goods and/or services and any operating or other expenses.

A key difficulty in measuring profit is in defining costs. Pure economic monetary profits can be zero or negative even in competitive equilibrium when accounted monetized costs exceed monetized price.

Chapter 3. Fundamental Principles of Value Creation

a. A Random Walk Down Wall Street
b. AAB
c. Economic profit
d. Accounting profit

6. In finance, _____ is the process of estimating the potential market value of a financial asset or liability. they can be done on assets (for example, investments in marketable securities such as stocks, options, business enterprises, or intangible assets such as patents and trademarks) or on liabilities (e.g., Bonds issued by a company.) _____s are required in many contexts including investment analysis, capital budgeting, merger and acquisition transactions, financial reporting, taxable events to determine the proper tax liability, and in litigation.
   a. Valuation
   b. Procter ' Gamble
   c. Margin
   d. Share

7. In finance, the _____ approach describes a method of valuing a project, company, or asset using the concepts of the time value of money. All future cash flows are estimated and discounted to give their present values. The discount rate used is generally the appropriate cost of capital and may incorporate judgments of the uncertainty (riskiness) of the future cash flows.
   a. Present value of benefits
   b. Discounted cash flow
   c. Net present value
   d. Future-oriented

8. _____ is the balance of the amounts of cash being received and paid by a business during a defined period of time, sometimes tied to a specific project. Measurement of _____ can be used

- to evaluate the state or performance of a business or project.
- to determine problems with liquidity. Being profitable does not necessarily mean being liquid. A company can fail because of a shortage of cash, even while profitable.
- to generate project rate of returns. The time of _____s into and out of projects are used as inputs to financial models such as internal rate of return, and net present value.
- to examine income or growth of a business when it is believed that accrual accounting concepts do not represent economic realities. Alternately, _____ can be used to 'validate' the net income generated by accrual accounting.

_____ as a generic term may be used differently depending on context, and certain _____ definitions may be adapted by analysts and users for their own uses. Common terms include operating _____ and free _____.

_____s can be classified into:

1. Operational _____s: Cash received or expended as a result of the company's core business activities.
2. Investment _____s: Cash received or expended through capital expenditure, investments or acquisitions.
3. Financing _____s: Cash received or expended as a result of financial activities, such as interests and dividends.

All three together - the net _____ - are necessary to reconcile the beginning cash balance to the ending cash balance. Loan draw downs or equity injections, that is just shifting of capital but no expenditure as such, are not considered in the net _____.

Chapter 3. Fundamental Principles of Value Creation

    a. Cash flow
    b. Shareholder value
    c. Corporate finance
    d. Real option

9. _____ or financing is to provide capital (funds), which means money for a project, a person, a business or any other private or public institutions.

Those funds can be allocated for either short term or long term purposes. The health fund is a new way of _____ private healthcare centers.

    a. Product life cycle
    b. Synthetic CDO
    c. Proxy fight
    d. Funding

10. The _____ is the rate that a company is expected to pay to finance its assets. WACC is the minimum return that a company must earn on existing asset base to satisfy its creditors, owners, and other providers of capital.

Companies raise money from a number of sources: common equity, preferred equity, straight debt, convertible debt, exchangeable debt, warrants, options, pension liabilities, executive stock options, governmental subsidies, and so on.

    a. Cost of capital
    b. 4-4-5 Calendar
    c. Capital intensity
    d. Weighted average cost of capital

11. _____ is an area of finance dealing with the financial decisions corporations make and the tools and analysis used to make these decisions. The primary goal of _____ is to maximize corporate value while managing the firm's financial risks. Although it is in principle different from managerial finance which studies the financial decisions of all firms, rather than corporations alone, the main concepts in the study of _____ are applicable to the financial problems of all kinds of firms.

    a. Cash flow
    b. Gross profit
    c. Special purpose entity
    d. Corporate finance

12. In economics, business, and accounting, a _____ is the value of money that has been used up to produce something, and hence is not available for use anymore. In business, the _____ may be one of acquisition, in which case the amount of money expended to acquire it is counted as _____. In this case, money is the input that is gone in order to acquire the thing.

    a. Fixed costs
    b. Sliding scale fees
    c. Marginal cost
    d. Cost

13. The _____ is an expected return that the provider of capital plans to earn on their investment.

Capital (money) used for funding a business should earn returns for the capital providers who risk their capital. For an investment to be worthwhile, the expected return on capital must be greater than the _____.

    a. Weighted average cost of capital
    b. 4-4-5 Calendar
    c. Cost of capital
    d. Capital intensity

Chapter 3. Fundamental Principles of Value Creation

14. In corporate finance, _____ is a cash flow available for distribution among all the security holders of a company. They include equity holders, debt holders, preferred stock holders, convertible security holders, and so on.

Note that the first three lines above are calculated for you on the standard Statement of Cash Flows.

a. Forfaiting
c. Safety stock

b. Free cash flow
d. Funding

Chapter 4. Do Fundamentals Really Drive the Stock Market?

1. A _____ is a private or public market for the trading of company stock and derivatives of company stock at an agreed price; these are securities listed on a stock exchange as well as those only traded privately.

The size of the world _____ is estimated at about $36.6 trillion US at the beginning of October 2008 . The world derivatives market has been estimated at about $480 trillion face or nominal value, 12 times the size of the entire world economy.

a. Adolph Coors
b. Anton Gelonkin
c. Andrew Tobias
d. Stock market

2. _____ is a business buzz term, which implies that the ultimate measure of a company's success is to enrich shareholders. It became popular during the 1980s, and is particularly associated with former CEO of General Electric, Jack Welch. In March 2009, Welch openly turned his back on the concept, calling _____ 'the dumbest idea in the world'.

For a publicly traded company, _____ is the part of its capitalization that is equity as opposed to long-term debt. In the case of only one type of stock, this would roughly be the number of outstanding shares times current shareprice. Things like dividends augment _____ while issuing of shares (stock options) lower it. This _____ added should be compared to average/required increase in value, aka cost of capital.

For a privately held company, the value of the firm after debt must be estimated using one of several valuation methods, s.a. discounted cash flow or others.

a. Cash flow
b. Commercial paper
c. Restricted stock
d. Shareholder value

3. In finance, _____ is the process of estimating the potential market value of a financial asset or liability. they can be done on assets (for example, investments in marketable securities such as stocks, options, business enterprises, or intangible assets such as patents and trademarks) or on liabilities (e.g., Bonds issued by a company.) _____s are required in many contexts including investment analysis, capital budgeting, merger and acquisition transactions, financial reporting, taxable events to determine the proper tax liability, and in litigation.

a. Valuation
b. Margin
c. Share
d. Procter ' Gamble

4. _____ is an accounting term used to reflect the portion of the book value of a business entity not directly attributable to its assets and liabilities; it normally arises only in case of an acquisition. It reflects the ability of the entity to make a higher profit than would be derived from selling the tangible assets. _____ is also known as an intangible asset.

a. Goodwill
b. Net profit
c. Cost of goods sold
d. Consolidation

5. The _____ on a portfolio of investments takes into account not only the capital appreciation on the portfolio, but also the income received on the portfolio. The income typically consists of interest, dividends, and securities lending fees. This contrasts with the price return, which takes into account only the capital gain on an investment.

a. Capitalization rate
b. Global tactical asset allocation
c. Profitability index
d. Total return

Chapter 4. Do Fundamentals Really Drive the Stock Market?

6. In economic models, the _____ time frame assumes no fixed factors of production. Firms can enter or leave the marketplace, and the cost (and availability) of land, labor, raw materials, and capital goods can be assumed to vary. In contrast, in the short-run time frame, certain factors are assumed to be fixed, because there is not sufficient time for them to change.
   a. 4-4-5 Calendar
   b. 529 plan
   c. Short-run
   d. Long-run

7. _____ are the earnings returned on the initial investment amount.

In the US, the Financial Accounting Standards Board (FASB) requires companies' income statements to report _____ for each of the major categories of the income statement: continuing operations, discontinued operations, extraordinary items, and net income.

The _____ formula does not include preferred dividends for categories outside of continued operations and net income.

   a. Earnings per share
   b. Average accounting return
   c. Inventory turnover
   d. Assets turnover

8. In business and finance, a _____ (also referred to as equity _____) of stock means a _____ of ownership in a corporation (company.) In the plural, stocks is often used as a synonym for _____s especially in the United States, but it is less commonly used that way outside of North America.

In the United Kingdom, South Africa, and Australia, stock can also refer to completely different financial instruments such as government bonds or, less commonly, to all kinds of marketable securities.

   a. Margin
   b. Bucket shop
   c. Share
   d. Procter ' Gamble

9. _____ are formal records of a business' financial activities.

_____ provide an overview of a business' financial condition in both short and long term. There are four basic _____:

   1. **Balance sheet**: also referred to as statement of financial position or condition, reports on a company's assets, liabilities, and net equity as of a given point in time.
   2. **Income statement**: also referred to as Profit and Loss statement (or a 'P'L'), reports on a company's income, expenses, and profits over a period of time.
   3. **Statement of retained earnings**: explains the changes in a company's retained earnings over the reporting period.
   4. **Statement of cash flows**: reports on a company's cash flow activities, particularly its operating, investing and financing activities.

Chapter 4. Do Fundamentals Really Drive the Stock Market?

a. Financial statements
b. Statement of retained earnings
c. Notes to the Financial Statements
d. Statement on Auditing Standards No. 70: Service Organizations

10. _____ is the standard framework of guidelines for financial accounting used in the United States of America. It includes the standards, conventions, and rules accountants follow in recording and summarizing transactions, and in the preparation of financial statements. _____ are now issued by the Financial Accounting Standards Board (FASB).
  a. Generally Accepted Accounting Principles
  b. Revenue
  c. Depreciation
  d. Net income

11. _____ is a list for goods and materials held available in stock by a business. It is also used for a list of the contents of a household and for a list for testamentary purposes of the possessions of someone who has died. In accounting _____ is considered an asset.
  a. AAB
  b. ABN Amro
  c. A Random Walk Down Wall Street
  d. Inventory

12. _____ methods are means of managing inventory and financial matters involving the money a company ties up within inventory of produced goods, raw materials, parts, components, or feed stocks.

In LIFO accounting, a historical method of recording the value of inventory, a firm records the last units purchased as the first units sold. LIFO is an acronym for 'last in, first out.' Sometimes the term FILO ('first in, last out') is used synonymously.

  a. Payroll
  b. General journal
  c. FIFO and LIFO accounting
  d. Net sales

13. The U.S. _____ is an independent agency of the United States government which holds primary responsibility for enforcing the federal securities laws and regulating the securities industry, the nation's stock and options exchanges, and other electronic securities markets. The SEC was created by section 4 of the SEC of 1934 (now codified as 15 U.S.C. Â§ 78d and commonly referred to as the 1934 Act.)
  a. 529 plan
  b. 7-Eleven
  c. 4-4-5 Calendar
  d. Securities and Exchange Commission

14. The term _____ describes a reduction in recognized value. In accounting terminology, it refers to recognition of the reduced or zero value of an asset. In income tax statements, it refers to a reduction of taxable income as recognition of certain expenses required to produce the income.
  a. Net profit
  b. Trial balance
  c. Write-off
  d. Net income

Chapter 4. Do Fundamentals Really Drive the Stock Market?

15. _____ is the process of decreasing an amount over a period of time. The word comes from Middle English amortisen to kill, alienate in mortmain, from Anglo-French amorteser, alteration of amortir, from Vulgar Latin admortire to kill, from Latin ad- + mort-, mors death. Particular instances of the term include:

- _____ (business), the allocation of a lump sum amount to different time periods, particularly for loans and other forms of finance, including related interest or other finance charges.
    - _____ schedule, a table detailing each periodic payment on a loan (typically a mortgage), as generated by an _____ calculator.
    - Negative _____, an _____ schedule where the loan amount actually increases through not paying the full interest
- Amortized analysis, analyzing the execution cost of algorithms over a sequence of operations.
- _____ of capital expenditures of certain assets under accounting rules, particularly intangible assets, in a manner analogous to depreciation.
- _____ (tax law)

_____ is also used in the context of zoning regulations and describes the time in which a property owner has to relocate when the property's use constitutes a preexisting nonconforming use under zoning regulations.

- Depreciation

a. Option
c. AT'T Inc.
b. Amortization
d. Intrinsic value

16. A _____ is the price of a single share of a no. of saleable stocks of the company. Once the stock is purchased, the owner becomes a shareholder of the company that issued the share.

a. Stock split
c. Whisper numbers
b. Share price
d. Trading curb

17. An _____ is a contract written by a seller that conveys to the buyer the right -- but not the obligation -- to buy (in the case of a call _____) or to sell (in the case of a put _____) a particular asset, such as a piece of property such as, among others, a futures contract. In return for granting the _____, the seller collects a payment (the premium) from the buyer.

For example, buying a call _____ provides the right to buy a specified quantity of a security at a set strike price at some time on or before expiration, while buying a put _____ provides the right to sell.

a. Annuity
c. AT'T Mobility LLC
b. Option
d. Amortization

18. In finance, _____ refers to the value of a security which is intrinsic to or contained in the security itself. It is also frequently called fundamental value. It is ordinarily calculated by summing the future income generated by the asset, and discounting it to the present value.

a. Intrinsic value
c. Alpha
b. Accretion
d. Amortization

Chapter 4. Do Fundamentals Really Drive the Stock Market?

19. A _____ rocket is a rocket that uses two or more stages, each of which contains its own engines and propellant. A tandem or serial stage is mounted on top of another stage; a parallel stage is attached alongside another stage. The result is effectively two or more rockets stacked on top of or attached next to each other.
   a. 4-4-5 Calendar
   b. 529 plan
   c. 7-Eleven
   d. Multistage

20. _____ is a finance term describing a firm's non-Equity cash flows. Theoretically, adding the discounted _____ to the discounted Flows to equity (also known as Equity Cash Flows) will give the firm's Enterprise Value. The Enterprise value is the valuation obtained by calculating the Discounted Cash Flow.
   a. Par value
   b. Debt cash flow
   c. Foreign exchange hedge
   d. Consignment stock

21. The institution most often referenced by the word '_____' is a public or publicly traded _____, the shares of which are traded on a public stock exchange (e.g., the New York Stock Exchange or Nasdaq in the United States) where shares of stock of _____s are bought and sold by and to the general public. Most of the largest businesses in the world are publicly traded _____s. However, the majority of _____s are said to be closely held, privately held or close _____s, meaning that no ready market exists for the trading of shares.
   a. Depository Trust Company
   b. Protect
   c. Federal Home Loan Mortgage Corporation
   d. Corporation

Chapter 5. Frameworks for Valuation

1. In finance, _____ is the process of estimating the potential market value of a financial asset or liability. they can be done on assets (for example, investments in marketable securities such as stocks, options, business enterprises, or intangible assets such as patents and trademarks) or on liabilities (e.g., Bonds issued by a company.) _____s are required in many contexts including investment analysis, capital budgeting, merger and acquisition transactions, financial reporting, taxable events to determine the proper tax liability, and in litigation.

   a. Margin
   b. Share
   c. Valuation
   d. Procter ' Gamble

2. _____ is a business valuation method. _____ is the net present value of a project if financed solely by ownership equity plus the present value of all the benefits of financing. Usually, the main benefit is a tax shield resulted from tax deductibility of interest payments. Another one can be a subsidized borrowing.

   a. AAB
   b. Adjusted present value
   c. ABN Amro
   d. A Random Walk Down Wall Street

3. The _____ is an expected return that the provider of capital plans to earn on their investment.

Capital (money) used for funding a business should earn returns for the capital providers who risk their capital. For an investment to be worthwhile, the expected return on capital must be greater than the _____.

   a. Cost of capital
   b. 4-4-5 Calendar
   c. Weighted average cost of capital
   d. Capital intensity

4. _____ is the balance of the amounts of cash being received and paid by a business during a defined period of time, sometimes tied to a specific project. Measurement of _____ can be used

   - to evaluate the state or performance of a business or project.
   - to determine problems with liquidity. Being profitable does not necessarily mean being liquid. A company can fail because of a shortage of cash, even while profitable.
   - to generate project rate of returns. The time of _____s into and out of projects are used as inputs to financial models such as internal rate of return, and net present value.
   - to examine income or growth of a business when it is believed that accrual accounting concepts do not represent economic realities. Alternately, _____ can be used to 'validate' the net income generated by accrual accounting.

_____ as a generic term may be used differently depending on context, and certain _____ definitions may be adapted by analysts and users for their own uses. Common terms include operating _____ and free _____.

_____s can be classified into:

   1. Operational _____s: Cash received or expended as a result of the company's core business activities.
   2. Investment _____s: Cash received or expended through capital expenditure, investments or acquisitions.
   3. Financing _____s: Cash received or expended as a result of financial activities, such as interests and dividends.

Chapter 5. Frameworks for Valuation

All three together - the net _____ - are necessary to reconcile the beginning cash balance to the ending cash balance. Loan draw downs or equity injections, that is just shifting of capital but no expenditure as such, are not considered in the net _____.

a. Corporate finance
c. Real option
b. Shareholder value
d. Cash flow

5. In economics, business, and accounting, a _____ is the value of money that has been used up to produce something, and hence is not available for use anymore. In business, the _____ may be one of acquisition, in which case the amount of money expended to acquire it is counted as _____. In this case, money is the input that is gone in order to acquire the thing.

a. Marginal cost
c. Sliding scale fees
b. Cost
d. Fixed costs

6. In finance, the _____ is the minimum rate of return a firm must offer shareholders to compensate for waiting for their returns, and for bearing some risk.

The _____ capital for a particular company is the rate of return on investment that is required by the company's ordinary shareholders. The return consists both of dividend and capital gains, e.g. increases in the share price.

a. Net pay
c. Cost of equity
b. Round-tripping
d. Residual value

7. _____ is the provision of resources (such as granting a loan) by one party to another party where that second party does not reimburse the first party immediately, thereby generating a debt, and instead arranges either to repay or return those resources (or material(s) of equal value) at a later date. The first party is called a creditor, also known as a lender, while the second party is called a debtor, also known as a borrower.

Movements of financial capital are normally dependent on either _____ or equity transfers.

a. Credit
c. Warrant
b. Comparable
d. Clearing house

8. A _____ assesses the credit worthiness of an individual, corporation, or even a country. _____s are calculated from financial history and current assets and liabilities. Typically, a _____ tells a lender or investor the probability of the subject being able to pay back a loan.

a. Credit cycle
c. Credit report monitoring
b. Debenture
d. Credit rating

9. A '_____' is a 'Charge' that is paid to obtain the right to delay a payment. Essentially, the payer purchases the right to make a given payment in the future instead of in the Present. The '_____', or 'Charge' that must be paid to delay the payment, is simply the difference between what the payment amount would be if it were paid in the present and what the payment amount would be paid if it were paid in the future.

a. Risk aversion
c. Risk modeling
b. Value at risk
d. Discount

10. The _____, P(T), is the number which a future cash flow, to be received at time T, must be multiplied by in order to obtain the current present value. Thus, a fixed annually compounded discount rate is

$$P(T) = \frac{1}{(1+r)^T}$$

For fixed continuously compounded discount rate we have

$$P(T) = e^{-rT}$$

For discounts in marketing, see discounts and allowances, sales promotion, and pricing.

a. Risk modeling
c. Risk premium
b. Discount
d. Discount factor

11. In finance, the _____ approach describes a method of valuing a project, company, or asset using the concepts of the time value of money. All future cash flows are estimated and discounted to give their present values. The discount rate used is generally the appropriate cost of capital and may incorporate judgments of the uncertainty (riskiness) of the future cash flows.
a. Future-oriented
c. Discounted cash flow
b. Net present value
d. Present value of benefits

12. Pure _____ is the increase in wealth that an investor has from making an investment, taking into consideration all costs associated with that investment including the opportunity cost of capital.

A key difficulty in measuring profit is in defining costs. Pure economic monetary profits can be zero or negative even in competitive equilibrium when accounted monetized costs exceed monetized price.

a. AAB
c. Operating profit
b. A Random Walk Down Wall Street
d. Economic profit

13. In corporate finance, _____ is a cash flow available for distribution among all the security holders of a company. They include equity holders, debt holders, preferred stock holders, convertible security holders, and so on.

Note that the first three lines above are calculated for you on the standard Statement of Cash Flows.

a. Safety stock
c. Funding
b. Forfaiting
d. Free cash flow

Chapter 5. Frameworks for Valuation

14. _____ is the value on a given date of a future payment or series of future payments, discounted to reflect the time value of money and other factors such as investment risk. _____ calculations are widely used in business and economics to provide a means to compare cash flows at different times on a meaningful 'like to like' basis.

The most commonly applied model of the time value of money is compound interest.

a. Net present value
c. Present value
b. Present value of benefits
d. Negative gearing

15. _____ is the difference between price and the costs of bringing to market whatever it is that is accounted as an enterprise (whether by harvest, extraction, manufacture, or purchase) in terms of the component costs of delivered goods and/or services and any operating or other expenses.

A key difficulty in measuring profit is in defining costs. Pure economic monetary profits can be zero or negative even in competitive equilibrium when accounted monetized costs exceed monetized price.

a. AAB
c. Economic profit
b. Accounting profit
d. A Random Walk Down Wall Street

16. _____ is a finance term describing a firm's non-Equity cash flows. Theoretically, adding the discounted _____ to the discounted Flows to equity (also known as Equity Cash Flows) will give the firm's Enterprise Value. The Enterprise value is the valuation obtained by calculating the Discounted Cash Flow.

a. Consignment stock
c. Foreign exchange hedge
b. Par value
d. Debt cash flow

17. _____ is a financial measure that quantifies how well a company generates cash flow relative to the capital it has invested in its business. It is defined as Net operating profit less adjusted taxes divided by Invested Capital and is usually expressed as a percentage. In this calculation, capital invested includes all monetary capital invested: long-term debt, common and preferred shares.

a. Cash conversion cycle
c. Debt service coverage ratio
b. Return on invested capital
d. Sharpe ratio

18. _____ represents the total cash investment that shareholders and debtholders have made in a company. There are two different but completely equivalent methods for calculating _____. The operating approach is calculated as:

_____ = Operating Net Working Capital + Net PP'E + Capitalized Operating Leases + Other Operating Assets + Operating Intangibles - Other Operating Liabilities - Cumulative Adjustment for Amortization of R'D

Equivalently, the financing approach is calculated as:

In symbols:

$$K = D + E - M$$

_____ is used in several important measurements of financial performance, including return on _____, economic value added, and free cash flow.

a. Information ratio
c. Operating leverage
b. Invested capital
d. Inventory turnover

19. The _____ is the rate that a company is expected to pay to finance its assets. WACC is the minimum return that a company must earn on existing asset base to satisfy its creditors, owners, and other providers of capital.

Companies raise money from a number of sources: common equity, preferred equity, straight debt, convertible debt, exchangeable debt, warrants, options, pension liabilities, executive stock options, governmental subsidies, and so on.

a. Cost of capital
c. 4-4-5 Calendar
b. Weighted average cost of capital
d. Capital intensity

20. A _____ is a fungible, negotiable instrument representing financial value. They are broadly categorized into debt securities (such as banknotes, bonds and debentures), and equity securities; e.g., common stocks. The company or other entity issuing the _____ is called the issuer.

a. Book entry
c. Security
b. Securities lending
d. Tracking stock

21. In business and accounting, _____s are everything of value that is owned by a person or company. The balance sheet of a firm records the monetary value of the _____s owned by the firm. The two major _____ classes are tangible _____s and intangible _____s.

a. EBITDA
c. Accounts payable
b. Asset
d. Income

22. _____ are securities that can be easily converted into cash. Such securities will generally have highly liquid markets allowing the security to be sold at a reasonable price very quickly. This is a usual feature in real estate.

a. Marketable
c. Securities lending
b. Tracking stock
d. Book entry

23. A _____, in business matters, is an entity that is controlled by a bigger and more powerful entity. The controlled entity is called a company, corporation, or limited liability company, and the controlling entity is called its parent (or the parent company.) The reason for this distinction is that a lone company cannot be a _____ of any organization; only an entity representing a legal fiction as a separate entity can be a _____.

a. Joint stock company
c. Subsidiary
b. 529 plan
d. 4-4-5 Calendar

24. _____ is that which is owed; usually referencing assets owed, but the term can cover other obligations. In the case of assets, _____ is a means of using future purchasing power in the present before a summation has been earned. Some companies and corporations use _____ as a part of their overall corporate finance strategy.

Chapter 5. Frameworks for Valuation

a. Debt
b. Partial Payment
c. Credit cycle
d. Cross-collateralization

25. An _____ is a call option on the common stock of a company, issued as a form of non-cash compensation. Restrictions on the option (such as vesting and limited transferability) attempt to align the holder's interest with those of the business' shareholders. If the company's stock rises, holders of options experience a direct financial benefit.
a. Internal financing
b. Operating ratio
c. Underwriting contract
d. Employee stock option

26. Leasing is a process by which a firm can obtain the use of a certain fixed assets for which it must pay a series of contractual, periodic, tax deductable payments. The lessee is the receiver of the services or the assets under the lease contract and the lessor is the owner of the assets. The relationship between the tenant and the landlord is called a _____, and can be for a fixed or an indefinite period of time (called the term of the lease.)
a. Real estate investing
b. Tenancy
c. Real Estate Investment Trust
d. REIT

27. In financial accounting, _____s are precautions for which the amount or probability of occurrence are not known. Typical examples are _____s for warranty costs and _____ for taxes the term reserve is used instead of term _____; such a use, however, is inconsistent with the terminology suggested by International Accounting Standards Board.
a. Money measurement concept
b. Provision
c. Petty cash
d. Momentum Accounting and Triple-Entry Bookkeeping

28. _____ are liabilities that may or may not be incurred by an entity depending on the outcome of a future event such as a court case. These liabilities are recorded in a company's accounts and shown in the balance sheet when both probable and reasonably estimable. A footnote to the balance sheet describes the nature and extent of the _____.
a. 4-4-5 Calendar
b. Due-on-sale clause
c. Contingent liabilities
d. 529 plan

29. An _____ is a lease whose term is short compared to the useful life of the asset or piece of equipment (an airliner, a ship etc.) being leased. An _____ is commonly used to acquire equipment on a relatively short-term basis.
a. A Random Walk Down Wall Street
b. ABN Amro
c. AAB
d. Operating lease

30. An _____ is a contract written by a seller that conveys to the buyer the right -- but not the obligation -- to buy (in the case of a call _____) or to sell (in the case of a put _____) a particular asset, such as a piece of property such as, among others, a futures contract. In return for granting the _____, the seller collects a payment (the premium) from the buyer.

For example, buying a call _____ provides the right to buy a specified quantity of a security at a set strike price at some time on or before expiration, while buying a put _____ provides the right to sell.

a. Annuity
b. AT'T Mobility LLC
c. Amortization
d. Option

Chapter 5. Frameworks for Valuation

31. _____ in business is an accounting concept that refers to ownership of a company (subsidiary) that is less than 50% of outstanding shares. _____ belongs to other investors and is reported on the consolidated balance sheet of the owning company to reflect the claim on assets belonging to other, non-controlling shareholders. Also, _____ is reported on the consolidated income statement as a share of profit belonging to minority shareholders.
   a. Fixed asset
   b. Construction in Progress
   c. Credit memo
   d. Minority interest

32. _____ is a fee paid on borrowed assets. It is the price paid for the use of borrowed money , or, money earned by deposited funds . Assets that are sometimes lent with _____ include money, shares, consumer goods through hire purchase, major assets such as aircraft, and even entire factories in finance lease arrangements.
   a. Interest
   b. Insolvency
   c. AAB
   d. A Random Walk Down Wall Street

33. In finance, _____ refers to the way a corporation finances its assets through some combination of equity, debt, or hybrid securities. A firm's _____ is then the composition or 'structure' of its liabilities. For example, a firm that sells $20 billion in equity and $80 billion in debt is said to be 20% equity-financed and 80% debt-financed.
   a. Book building
   b. Rights issue
   c. Market for corporate control
   d. Capital structure

34. A _____ is the reduction in income taxes that results from taking an allowable deduction from taxable income. For example, because interest on debt is a tax-deductible expense, taking on debt creates a _____. Since a _____ is a way to save cash flows, it increases the value of the business, and it is an important aspect of business valuation.
   a. Refinancing risk
   b. Present value of costs
   c. Tax shield
   d. Present value of benefits

35. The _____ is an interest rate a central bank charges depository institutions that borrow reserves from it.

The term _____ has two meanings:

- the same as interest rate; the term 'discount' does not refer to the meaning of the word, but to the purpose of using the quantity, such as computations of present value, e.g. net present value / discounted cash flow

- the annual effective _____, which is the annual interest divided by the capital including that interest; this rate is lower than the interest rate; it corresponds to using the value after a year as the nominal value, and seeing the initial value as the nominal value minus a discount; it is used for Treasury Bills and similar financial instruments

The annual effective _____ is the annual interest divided by the capital including that interest, which is the interest rate divided by 100% plus the interest rate. It is the annual discount factor to be applied to the future cash flow, to find the discount, subtracted from a future value to find the value one year earlier.

For example, suppose there is a government bond that sells for $95 and pays $100 in a year's time.

   a. Stochastic volatility
   b. Fisher equation
   c. Black-Scholes
   d. Discount rate

Chapter 5. Frameworks for Valuation

36. _____ is an acronym that refers to a company's earnings before the deduction of interest, tax and amortization expenses. It is a financial indicator used widely as a measure of efficiency and profitability.
a. ABN Amro
b. A Random Walk Down Wall Street
c. EBITA
d. AAB

37. In corporate finance, _____ analysis applies put option and call option valuation techniques to capital budgeting decisions. A _____ itself, is the right--but not the obligation--to undertake some business decision; typically the option to make, or abandon, a capital investment. For example, the opportunity to invest in the expansion of a firm's factory, or alternatively to sell the factory, is a _____.
a. Cash flow
b. Capital budgeting
c. Book building
d. Real option

38. _____ is one of the authors of the Black-Scholes equation. In 1997 he was awarded the Nobel Memorial Prize in Economic Sciences for 'a new method to determine the value of derivatives'. The model provides the fundamental conceptual framework for valuing options, such as calls or puts, and is referred to as the Black-Scholes model, which has become the standard in financial markets globally.
a. Robert James Shiller
b. Adolph Coors
c. Myron Samuel Scholes
d. Andrew Tobias

39. _____ is the process of decreasing an amount over a period of time. The word comes from Middle English amortisen to kill, alienate in mortmain, from Anglo-French amorteser, alteration of amortir, from Vulgar Latin admortire to kill, from Latin ad- + mort-, mors death. Particular instances of the term include:

- _____ (business), the allocation of a lump sum amount to different time periods, particularly for loans and other forms of finance, including related interest or other finance charges.
  - _____ schedule, a table detailing each periodic payment on a loan (typically a mortgage), as generated by an _____ calculator.
  - Negative _____, an _____ schedule where the loan amount actually increases through not paying the full interest
- Amortized analysis, analyzing the execution cost of algorithms over a sequence of operations.
- _____ of capital expenditures of certain assets under accounting rules, particularly intangible assets, in a manner analogous to depreciation.
- _____ (tax law)

_____ is also used in the context of zoning regulations and describes the time in which a property owner has to relocate when the property's use constitutes a preexisting nonconforming use under zoning regulations.

- Depreciation

a. Intrinsic value
b. AT'T Inc.
c. Amortization
d. Option

Chapter 6. Thinking about Return on Invested Capital and Growth

1. In economics, business, and accounting, a _____ is the value of money that has been used up to produce something, and hence is not available for use anymore. In business, the _____ may be one of acquisition, in which case the amount of money expended to acquire it is counted as _____. In this case, money is the input that is gone in order to acquire the thing.
   a. Fixed costs
   b. Marginal cost
   c. Sliding scale fees
   d. Cost

2. _____ is an accounting term used to reflect the portion of the book value of a business entity not directly attributable to its assets and liabilities; it normally arises only in case of an acquisition. It reflects the ability of the entity to make a higher profit than would be derived from selling the tangible assets. _____ is also known as an intangible asset.
   a. Cost of goods sold
   b. Goodwill
   c. Consolidation
   d. Net profit

3. _____ represents the total cash investment that shareholders and debtholders have made in a company. There are two different but completely equivalent methods for calculating _____. The operating approach is calculated as:

   _____ = Operating Net Working Capital + Net PP'E + Capitalized Operating Leases + Other Operating Assets + Operating Intangibles - Other Operating Liabilities - Cumulative Adjustment for Amortization of R'D

   Equivalently, the financing approach is calculated as:

   In symbols:

   $$K = D + E - M$$

   _____ is used in several important measurements of financial performance, including return on _____, economic value added, and free cash flow.

   a. Inventory turnover
   b. Operating leverage
   c. Information ratio
   d. Invested capital

4. _____ is a financial measure that quantifies how well a company generates cash flow relative to the capital it has invested in its business. It is defined as Net operating profit less adjusted taxes divided by Invested Capital and is usually expressed as a percentage. In this calculation, capital invested includes all monetary capital invested: long-term debt, common and preferred shares.
   a. Sharpe ratio
   b. Debt service coverage ratio
   c. Cash conversion cycle
   d. Return on invested capital

5. In business, _____ is income that a company receives from its normal business activities, usually from the sale of goods and services to customers. Some companies also receive _____ from interest, dividends or royalties paid to them by other companies. _____ may refer to business income in general, or it may refer to the amount, in a monetary unit, received during a period of time, as in 'Last year, Company X had _____ of $32 million.'

   In many countries, including the UK, _____ is referred to as turnover.

a. Bottom line
c. Furniture, Fixtures and Equipment
b. Matching principle
d. Revenue

6. P is a stochastic matrix, which is an important fact to keep in mind for the rest of this discussion. If the Markov chain is time-homogeneous, then the transition matrix P is the same after each step, so the k-step _____ can be computed as the k-th power of the transition matrix, P^k.

The stationary distribution π is a (row) vector whose entries sum to 1 that satisfies the equation

$$\pi = \pi \mathbf{P}.$$

In other words, the stationary distribution π is a normalized (meaning that the sum of its entries is 1) left eigenvector of the transition matrix associated with the eigenvalue 1.

a. Transition probability
c. 7-Eleven
b. 4-4-5 Calendar
d. 529 plan

7. _____ is the balance of the amounts of cash being received and paid by a business during a defined period of time, sometimes tied to a specific project. Measurement of _____ can be used

- to evaluate the state or performance of a business or project.
- to determine problems with liquidity. Being profitable does not necessarily mean being liquid. A company can fail because of a shortage of cash, even while profitable.
- to generate project rate of returns. The time of _____s into and out of projects are used as inputs to financial models such as internal rate of return, and net present value.
- to examine income or growth of a business when it is believed that accrual accounting concepts do not represent economic realities. Alternately, _____ can be used to 'validate' the net income generated by accrual accounting.

_____ as a generic term may be used differently depending on context, and certain _____ definitions may be adapted by analysts and users for their own uses. Common terms include operating _____ and free _____.

_____s can be classified into:

1. Operational _____s: Cash received or expended as a result of the company's core business activities.
2. Investment _____s: Cash received or expended through capital expenditure, investments or acquisitions.
3. Financing _____s: Cash received or expended as a result of financial activities, such as interests and dividends.

All three together - the net _____ - are necessary to reconcile the beginning cash balance to the ending cash balance. Loan draw downs or equity injections, that is just shifting of capital but no expenditure as such, are not considered in the net _____.

a. Shareholder value
b. Corporate finance
c. Real option
d. Cash flow

8. In corporate finance, _____ is a cash flow available for distribution among all the security holders of a company. They include equity holders, debt holders, preferred stock holders, convertible security holders, and so on.

Note that the first three lines above are calculated for you on the standard Statement of Cash Flows.

a. Forfaiting
b. Free cash flow
c. Safety stock
d. Funding

Chapter 7. Analyzing Historical Performance

1. In financial accounting, a _____ or statement of financial position is a summary of a person's or organization's balances. Assets, liabilities and ownership equity are listed as of a specific date, such as the end of its financial year. A _____ is often described as a snapshot of a company's financial condition.

   a. Financial statements
   b. Statement of retained earnings
   c. Balance sheet
   d. Statement on Auditing Standards No. 70: Service Organizations

2. _____ is the balance of the amounts of cash being received and paid by a business during a defined period of time, sometimes tied to a specific project. Measurement of _____ can be used

   - to evaluate the state or performance of a business or project.
   - to determine problems with liquidity. Being profitable does not necessarily mean being liquid. A company can fail because of a shortage of cash, even while profitable.
   - to generate project rate of returns. The time of _____s into and out of projects are used as inputs to financial models such as internal rate of return, and net present value.
   - to examine income or growth of a business when it is believed that accrual accounting concepts do not represent economic realities. Alternately, _____ can be used to 'validate' the net income generated by accrual accounting.

   _____ as a generic term may be used differently depending on context, and certain _____ definitions may be adapted by analysts and users for their own uses. Common terms include operating _____ and free _____.

   _____s can be classified into:

   1. Operational _____s: Cash received or expended as a result of the company's core business activities.
   2. Investment _____s: Cash received or expended through capital expenditure, investments or acquisitions.
   3. Financing _____s: Cash received or expended as a result of financial activities, such as interests and dividends.

   All three together - the net _____ - are necessary to reconcile the beginning cash balance to the ending cash balance. Loan draw downs or equity injections, that is just shifting of capital but no expenditure as such, are not considered in the net _____.

   a. Real option
   b. Corporate finance
   c. Shareholder value
   d. Cash flow

3. _____ are formal records of a business' financial activities.

Chapter 7. Analyzing Historical Performance

_____ provide an overview of a business' financial condition in both short and long term. There are four basic _____:

1. **Balance sheet**: also referred to as statement of financial position or condition, reports on a company's assets, liabilities, and net equity as of a given point in time.
2. **Income statement**: also referred to as Profit and Loss statement (or a 'P'L'), reports on a company's income, expenses, and profits over a period of time.
3. **Statement of retained earnings**: explains the changes in a company's retained earnings over the reporting period.
4. **Statement of cash flows**: reports on a company's cash flow activities, particularly its operating, investing and financing activities.

a. Statement of retained earnings

b. Statement on Auditing Standards No. 70: Service Organizations

c. Notes to the Financial Statements

d. Financial statements

4. _____, refers to consumption opportunity gained by an entity within a specified time frame, which is generally expressed in monetary terms. However, for households and individuals, '_____ is the sum of all the wages, salaries, profits, interests payments, rents and other forms of earnings received... in a given period of time.' For firms, _____ generally refers to net-profit: what remains of revenue after expenses have been subtracted.

a. OIBDA

b. Annual report

c. Accrual

d. Income

5. An _____ is a financial statement for companies that indicates how Revenue is transformed into net income The purpose of the _____ is to show managers and investors whether the company made or lost money during the period being reported.

The important thing to remember about an _____ is that it represents a period of time.

a. AAB

b. ABN Amro

c. A Random Walk Down Wall Street

d. Income statement

6. _____ = net operating profit less adjusted taxes.

Used in preference to Net Income as it removes the effects of capital structure (debt vs. equity.) The Operating Profit is prior to interest and taxes being subtracted, which makes _____ equal NOPAT.

a. NOPLAT

b. Flight-to-quality

c. Consolidated financial statements

d. Coupon leverage

7. _____ represents the total cash investment that shareholders and debtholders have made in a company. There are two different but completely equivalent methods for calculating _____. The operating approach is calculated as:

Chapter 7. Analyzing Historical Performance

_____ = Operating Net Working Capital + Net PP'E + Capitalized Operating Leases + Other Operating Assets + Operating Intangibles - Other Operating Liabilities - Cumulative Adjustment for Amortization of R'D

Equivalently, the financing approach is calculated as:

In symbols:

$$K = D + E - M$$

_____ is used in several important measurements of financial performance, including return on _____, economic value added, and free cash flow.

a. Invested capital
b. Inventory turnover
c. Information ratio
d. Operating leverage

8. In business and accounting, _____s are everything of value that is owned by a person or company. The balance sheet of a firm records the monetary value of the _____s owned by the firm. The two major _____ classes are tangible _____s and intangible _____s.
   a. EBITDA
   b. Income
   c. Asset
   d. Accounts payable

9. In corporate finance, _____ is a cash flow available for distribution among all the security holders of a company. They include equity holders, debt holders, preferred stock holders, convertible security holders, and so on.

Note that the first three lines above are calculated for you on the standard Statement of Cash Flows.

   a. Forfaiting
   b. Funding
   c. Safety stock
   d. Free cash flow

10. _____ is a finance term describing a firm's non-Equity cash flows. Theoretically, adding the discounted _____ to the discounted Flows to equity (also known as Equity Cash Flows) will give the firm's Enterprise Value. The Enterprise value is the valuation obtained by calculating the Discounted Cash Flow.
    a. Debt cash flow
    b. Consignment stock
    c. Foreign exchange hedge
    d. Par value

11. _____ is a financial metric which represents operating liquidity available to a business. Along with fixed assets such as plant and equipment, _____ is considered a part of operating capital. It is calculated as current assets minus current liabilities.
    a. 529 plan
    b. 4-4-5 Calendar
    c. Working capital management
    d. Working capital

Chapter 7. Analyzing Historical Performance

12. _____ are defined as identifiable non-monetary assets that cannot be seen, touched or physically measured, which are created through time and/or effort and that are identifiable as a separate asset. There are two primary forms of intangibles - legal intangibles (such as trade secrets (e.g., customer lists), copyrights, patents, trademarks, and goodwill) and competitive intangibles (such as knowledge activities (know-how, knowledge), collaboration activities, leverage activities, and structural activities.) Legal intangibles generate legal property rights defensible in a court of law.

   a. AAB
   b. Intangible assets
   c. A Random Walk Down Wall Street
   d. ABN Amro

13. _____ is a measure of a company's earning power from ongoing operations, equal to earnings before the deduction of interest payments and income taxes.

To accountants, economic profit, or EP, is a single-period metric to determine the value created by a company in one period - usually a year. It is the net profit after tax less the equity charge, a risk-weighted cost of capital.

   a. Economic profit
   b. A Random Walk Down Wall Street
   c. Operating profit
   d. AAB

14. _____ is the difference between price and the costs of bringing to market whatever it is that is accounted as an enterprise (whether by harvest, extraction, manufacture, or purchase) in terms of the component costs of delivered goods and/or services and any operating or other expenses.

A key difficulty in measuring profit is in defining costs. Pure economic monetary profits can be zero or negative even in competitive equilibrium when accounted monetized costs exceed monetized price.

   a. AAB
   b. Economic profit
   c. A Random Walk Down Wall Street
   d. Accounting profit

15. The phrase _____ according to the Organization for Economic Co-operation and Development, refers to 'creative work undertaken on a systematic basis in order to increase the stock of knowledge, including knowledge of (hu)man, culture and society, and the use of this stock of knowledge to devise new applications'.

New product design and development is more than often a crucial factor in the survival of a company. In an industry that is fast changing, firms must continually revise their design and range of products. This is necessary due to continuous technology change and development as well as other competitors and the changing preference of customers.

   a. 7-Eleven
   b. 4-4-5 Calendar
   c. 529 plan
   d. Research and development

16. An _____ is quite usually a standard guarantee from the seller of a product that specifies the extent to which the quality or performance of the product is assured and states the conditions under which the product can be returned, replaced, or repaired. It is often given in the form of a specific, written 'Warranty' document. However, a warranty may also arise by operation of law based upon the seller's description of the goods, and perhaps their source and quality, and any material deviation from that specification would violate the guarantee.

Chapter 7. Analyzing Historical Performance

    a. Economies of scale   b. Assumption of risk
    c. Economic depreciation   d. Express warranty

17. A _____ is a fungible, negotiable instrument representing financial value. They are broadly categorized into debt securities (such as banknotes, bonds and debentures), and equity securities; e.g., common stocks. The company or other entity issuing the _____ is called the issuer.
    a. Book entry   b. Securities lending
    c. Tracking stock   d. Security

18. A _____, in business matters, is an entity that is controlled by a bigger and more powerful entity. The controlled entity is called a company, corporation, or limited liability company, and the controlling entity is called its parent (or the parent company.) The reason for this distinction is that a lone company cannot be a _____ of any organization; only an entity representing a legal fiction as a separate entity can be a _____.
    a. Subsidiary   b. Joint stock company
    c. 529 plan   d. 4-4-5 Calendar

19. _____ are securities that can be easily converted into cash. Such securities will generally have highly liquid markets allowing the security to be sold at a reasonable price very quickly. This is a usual feature in real estate.
    a. Book entry   b. Tracking stock
    c. Securities lending   d. Marketable

20. _____ is that which is owed; usually referencing assets owed, but the term can cover other obligations. In the case of assets, _____ is a means of using future purchasing power in the present before a summation has been earned. Some companies and corporations use _____ as a part of their overall corporate finance strategy.
    a. Cross-collateralization   b. Credit cycle
    c. Partial Payment   d. Debt

21. Leasing is a process by which a firm can obtain the use of a certain fixed assets for which it must pay a series of contractual, periodic, tax deductable payments. The lessee is the receiver of the services or the assets under the lease contract and the lessor is the owner of the assets. The relationship between the tenant and the landlord is called a _____, and can be for a fixed or an indefinite period of time (called the term of the lease.)
    a. Real estate investing   b. REIT
    c. Real Estate Investment Trust   d. Tenancy

22. In economics, business, and accounting, a _____ is the value of money that has been used up to produce something, and hence is not available for use anymore. In business, the _____ may be one of acquisition, in which case the amount of money expended to acquire it is counted as _____. In this case, money is the input that is gone in order to acquire the thing.
    a. Marginal cost   b. Fixed costs
    c. Sliding scale fees   d. Cost

23. In finance, the _____ is the minimum rate of return a firm must offer shareholders to compensate for waiting for their returns, and for bearing some risk.

Chapter 7. Analyzing Historical Performance

The _____ capital for a particular company is the rate of return on investment that is required by the company's ordinary shareholders. The return consists both of dividend and capital gains, e.g. increases in the share price.

a. Net pay
b. Residual value
c. Round-tripping
d. Cost of equity

24. _____ is a subsection in equity where 'other comprehensive income' is accumulated (summed or 'aggregated'.)

The balance of _____ is presented in the Equity section of the Balance Sheet as is the Retained Earnings balance, which aggregates past and current Earnings, and past and current Dividends.

Other comprehensive income is the difference between net income and comprehensive income and represents the certain gains and losses of the enterprise.

a. ABN Amro
b. AAB
c. A Random Walk Down Wall Street
d. Accumulated other comprehensive income

25. In finance, _____ refers to the way a corporation finances its assets through some combination of equity, debt, or hybrid securities. A firm's _____ is then the composition or 'structure' of its liabilities. For example, a firm that sells $20 billion in equity and $80 billion in debt is said to be 20% equity-financed and 80% debt-financed.

a. Capital structure
b. Book building
c. Market for corporate control
d. Rights issue

26. _____ is a specific term used in companies' financial reporting from the company-whole point of view. Because that use excludes the effects of changing ownership interest, an economic measure of _____ is necessary for financial analysis from the shareholders' point of view

_____ is defined by the Financial Accounting Standards Board, or FASB, as 'e;the change in equity [net assets] of a business enterprise during a period from transactions and other events and circumstances from nonowner sources. It includes all changes in equity during a period except those resulting from investments by owners and distributions to owners.'e;

_____ is the sum of net income and other items that must bypass the income statement because they have not been realized, including items like an unrealized holding gain or loss from available for sale securities and foreign currency translation gains or losses.

a. 529 plan
b. 4-4-5 Calendar
c. Comprehensive income
d. 7-Eleven

27. _____, in accrual accounting, is any account where the asset or liability is not realized until a future date, e.g. annuities, charges, taxes, income, etc. The _____ item may be carried, dependent on type of deferral, as either an asset or liability.See also: accrual

_____ is also used in the university admissions process. It is the action by which a school rejects a student for early admission but still opts to review that student in the general admissions pool.

a. Net profit
c. Deferred
b. Revenue
d. Current asset

28. _____ is an accounting concept, meaning a future tax liability or asset, resulting from temporary differences between book (accounting) value of assets and liabilities and their tax value, or timing differences between the recognition of gains and losses in financial statements and their recognition in a tax computation.

Temporary differences are differences between the carrying amount of an asset or liability recognised in the balance sheet and the amount attributed to that asset or liability for tax purposes (the tax base.)

Temporary differences may be either:

- taxable temporary differences, which are temporary differences that will result in taxable amounts in determining taxable profit (tax loss) of future periods when the carrying amount of the asset or liability is recovered or settled; or
- deductible temporary differences, which are temporary differences that will result in deductible amounts in determining taxable profit (tax loss) of future periods when the carrying amount of the asset or liability is recovered or settled.

The tax base of an asset or liability is the amount attributed to that asset or liability for tax purposes:

- the tax base of an asset is the amount that will be deductible for tax purposes against any taxable economic benefits that will flow to an entity when it recovers the carrying amount of the asset.

- the tax base of a liability is its carrying amount, less any amount that will be deductible for tax purposes in respect of that liability in future periods.

The basic principle of accounting for _____ under a temporary difference approach can be illustrated using a common example in which a company has fixed assets which qualify for tax depreciation.

a. Qualified residence interest
c. Tax exemption
b. Monetary policy
d. Deferred Tax

29. _____ is an acronym that refers to a company's earnings before the deduction of interest, tax and amortization expenses. It is a financial indicator used widely as a measure of efficiency and profitability.
a. ABN Amro
c. A Random Walk Down Wall Street
b. AAB
d. EBITA

30. An _____ is a lease whose term is short compared to the useful life of the asset or piece of equipment (an airliner, a ship etc.) being leased. An _____ is commonly used to acquire equipment on a relatively short-term basis.

Chapter 7. Analyzing Historical Performance

a. ABN Amro
b. Operating lease
c. A Random Walk Down Wall Street
d. AAB

31. _____ is equal to the income that a firm has after subtracting costs and expenses from the total revenue. _____ can be distributed among holders of common stock as a dividend or held by the firm as retained earnings. _____ is an accounting term; in some countries (such as the UK) profit is the usual term.
   a. Historical cost
   b. Write-off
   c. Furniture, Fixtures and Equipment
   d. Net income

32. A _____ is an expenditure creating future benefits. A _____ is incurred when a business spends money either to buy fixed assets or to add to the value of an existing fixed asset with a useful life that extends beyond the taxable year. Capex are used by a company to acquire or upgrade physical assets such as equipment, property, or industrial buildings.
   a. Weighted average cost of capital
   b. Capital expenditure
   c. Cost of capital
   d. 4-4-5 Calendar

33. An _____, operating expenditure, operational expense, operational expenditure or OPEX is an on-going cost for running a product, business, or system. Its counterpart, a capital expenditure (CAPEX), is the cost of developing or providing non-consumable parts for the product or system. For example, the purchase of a photocopier is the CAPEX, and the annual paper and toner cost is the OPEX.
   a. AAB
   b. ABN Amro
   c. A Random Walk Down Wall Street
   d. Operating expense

34. An _____ is a contract written by a seller that conveys to the buyer the right -- but not the obligation -- to buy (in the case of a call _____) or to sell (in the case of a put _____) a particular asset, such as a piece of property such as, among others, a futures contract. In return for granting the _____, the seller collects a payment (the premium) from the buyer.

For example, buying a call _____ provides the right to buy a specified quantity of a security at a set strike price at some time on or before expiration, while buying a put _____ provides the right to sell.

   a. Option
   b. Annuity
   c. AT'T Mobility LLC
   d. Amortization

35. _____ or fair value accounting refers to the accounting standards of assigning a value to a position held in a financial instrument based on the current fair market price for the instrument or similar instruments. Fair value accounting has been a part of US Generally Accepted Accounting Principles (GAAP) since the early 1990s. The use of fair value measurements has increased steadily over the past decade, primarily in response to investor demand for relevant and timely financial statements that will aid in making better informed decisions.
   a. 529 plan
   b. 7-Eleven
   c. 4-4-5 Calendar
   d. Mark-to-market

36. _____ is a fee paid on borrowed assets. It is the price paid for the use of borrowed money, or, money earned by deposited funds. Assets that are sometimes lent with _____ include money, shares, consumer goods through hire purchase, major assets such as aircraft, and even entire factories in finance lease arrangements.

Chapter 7. Analyzing Historical Performance

a. Interest
b. AAB
c. Insolvency
d. A Random Walk Down Wall Street

37. In business and finance, a _____ (also referred to as equity _____) of stock means a _____ of ownership in a corporation (company.) In the plural, stocks is often used as a synonym for _____s especially in the United States, but it is less commonly used that way outside of North America.

In the United Kingdom, South Africa, and Australia, stock can also refer to completely different financial instruments such as government bonds or, less commonly, to all kinds of marketable securities.

a. Margin
b. Bucket shop
c. Procter ' Gamble
d. Share

38. In some countries, including the United States and the United Kingdom, corporations can buy back their own stock in a share repurchase, also known as a _____ or share buyback. There has been a meteoric rise in the use of share repurchases in the U.S. in the past twenty years, from $5b in 1980 to $349b in 2005. A share repurchase distributes cash to existing shareholders in exchange for a fraction of the firm's outstanding equity.

a. Stock repurchase
b. Trading curb
c. Common stock
d. Stockholder

39. _____, _____ includes the direct costs attributable to the production of the goods sold by a company. This amount includes the materials cost used in creating the goods along with the direct labor costs used to produce the good. It excludes indirect expenses such as distribution costs and sales force costs.

a. Net profit
b. Goodwill
c. Cost of goods sold
d. Deferred financing costs

40. Pure _____ is the increase in wealth that an investor has from making an investment, taking into consideration all costs associated with that investment including the opportunity cost of capital.

A key difficulty in measuring profit is in defining costs. Pure economic monetary profits can be zero or negative even in competitive equilibrium when accounted monetized costs exceed monetized price.

a. A Random Walk Down Wall Street
b. Economic profit
c. AAB
d. Operating profit

41. _____ methods are means of managing inventory and financial matters involving the money a company ties up within inventory of produced goods, raw materials, parts, components, or feed stocks.

In LIFO accounting, a historical method of recording the value of inventory, a firm records the last units purchased as the first units sold. LIFO is an acronym for 'last in, first out.' Sometimes the term FILO ('first in, last out') is used synonymously.

a. General journal
b. Payroll
c. FIFO and LIFO accounting
d. Net sales

42. In business, _____ is income that a company receives from its normal business activities, usually from the sale of goods and services to customers. Some companies also receive _____ from interest, dividends or royalties paid to them by other companies. _____ may refer to business income in general, or it may refer to the amount, in a monetary unit, received during a period of time, as in 'Last year, Company X had _____ of $32 million.'

In many countries, including the UK, _____ is referred to as turnover.

a. Furniture, Fixtures and Equipment
b. Matching principle
c. Revenue
d. Bottom line

43. Times interest earned (TIE) or _____ is a measure of a company's ability to honor its debt payments. It may be calculated as either EBIT or EBITDA divided by the total interest payable.

$$\text{Times-Interest-Earned} = \frac{\text{EBIT or EBITDA}}{\text{Interest Charges}}$$

- Financial ratio
- Financial leverage
- EBIT
- EBITDA
- Debt service coverage ratio

Interest Charges = Traditionally 'charges' refers to interest expense found on the income statement.

Times Interest Earned or Interest Coverage is a great tool when measuring a company's ability to meet its debt obligations.

a. Interest coverage ratio
b. Earnings per share
c. Assets turnover
d. Information ratio

44. _____ is the process of decreasing an amount over a period of time. The word comes from Middle English amortisen to kill, alienate in mortmain, from Anglo-French amorteser, alteration of amortir, from Vulgar Latin admortire to kill, from Latin ad- + mort-, mors death. Particular instances of the term include:

- _____ (business), the allocation of a lump sum amount to different time periods, particularly for loans and other forms of finance, including related interest or other finance charges.
   o _____ schedule, a table detailing each periodic payment on a loan (typically a mortgage), as generated by an _____ calculator.
   o Negative _____, an _____ schedule where the loan amount actually increases through not paying the full interest
- Amortized analysis, analyzing the execution cost of algorithms over a sequence of operations.
- _____ of capital expenditures of certain assets under accounting rules, particularly intangible assets, in a manner analogous to depreciation.
- _____ (tax law)

_____ is also used in the context of zoning regulations and describes the time in which a property owner has to relocate when the property's use constitutes a preexisting nonconforming use under zoning regulations.

- Depreciation

a. AT'T Inc.   b. Amortization
c. Option   d. Intrinsic value

45. _____ is the provision of resources (such as granting a loan) by one party to another party where that second party does not reimburse the first party immediately, thereby generating a debt, and instead arranges either to repay or return those resources (or material(s) of equal value) at a later date. The first party is called a creditor, also known as a lender, while the second party is called a debtor, also known as a borrower.

Movements of financial capital are normally dependent on either _____ or equity transfers.

a. Comparable   b. Clearing house
c. Warrant   d. Credit

46. _____ is a term used in accounting, economics and finance to spread the cost of an asset over the span of several years.

In simple words we can say that _____ is the reduction in the value of an asset due to usage, passage of time, wear and tear, technological outdating or obsolescence, depletion or other such factors.

In accounting, _____ is a term used to describe any method of attributing the historical or purchase cost of an asset across its useful life, roughly corresponding to normal wear and tear.

a. Matching principle   b. Deferred financing costs
c. Bottom line   d. Depreciation

47. A _____ assesses the credit worthiness of an individual, corporation, or even a country. _____s are calculated from financial history and current assets and liabilities. Typically, a _____ tells a lender or investor the probability of the subject being able to pay back a loan.
a. Debenture   b. Credit rating
c. Credit report monitoring   d. Credit cycle

48. In finance, _____ (or gearing) is borrowing money to supplement existing funds for investment in such a way that the potential positive or negative outcome is magnified and/or enhanced. It generally refers to using borrowed funds, or debt, so as to attempt to increase the returns to equity. Deleveraging is the action of reducing borrowings.
a. Leverage   b. Limited partnership
c. Financial endowment   d. Pension fund

49. _____ is the fraction of net income a firm pays to its stockholders in dividends:

Chapter 7. Analyzing Historical Performance

The part of the earnings not paid to investors is left for investment to provide for future earnings growth. Investors seeking high current income and limited capital growth prefer companies with high _____. However investors seeking capital growth may prefer lower payout ratio because capital gains are taxed at a lower rate.

a. Dividend imputation
b. Dividend yield
c. Dividend puzzle
d. Dividend payout ratio

50. An _____ is a call option on the common stock of a company, issued as a form of non-cash compensation. Restrictions on the option (such as vesting and limited transferability) attempt to align the holder's interest with those of the business' shareholders. If the company's stock rises, holders of options experience a direct financial benefit.
a. Internal financing
b. Operating ratio
c. Underwriting contract
d. Employee stock option

51. In financial accounting, _____s are precautions for which the amount or probability of occurrence are not known. Typical examples are _____s for warranty costs and _____ for taxes the term reserve is used instead of term _____; such a use, however, is inconsistent with the terminology suggested by International Accounting Standards Board.
a. Petty cash
b. Momentum Accounting and Triple-Entry Bookkeeping
c. Money measurement concept
d. Provision

52. In economic models, the _____ time frame assumes no fixed factors of production. Firms can enter or leave the marketplace, and the cost (and availability) of land, labor, raw materials, and capital goods can be assumed to vary. In contrast, in the short-run time frame, certain factors are assumed to be fixed, because there is not sufficient time for them to change.
a. 4-4-5 Calendar
b. Short-run
c. 529 plan
d. Long-run

53. In financial accounting, the term _____ is most commonly used to describe any part of shareholders' equity, except for basic share capital. Sometimes, the term is used instead of the term provision; such a use, however, is inconsistent with the terminology suggested by International Accounting Standards Board. For more information about provisions, see provision (accounting.)
a. Treasury stock
b. Closing entries
c. FIFO and LIFO accounting
d. Reserve

54. In statistics and image processing, to smooth a data set is to create an approximating function that attempts to capture important patterns in the data, while leaving out noise or other fine-scale structures/rapid phenomena. Many different algorithms are used in _____. One of the most common algorithms is the 'moving average', often used to try to capture important trends in repeated statistical surveys.
a. 7-Eleven
b. 529 plan
c. 4-4-5 Calendar
d. Smoothing

Chapter 7. Analyzing Historical Performance

55. _____ is the corporate management term for the act of reorganizing the legal, ownership, operational, or other structures of a company for the purpose of making it more profitable or better organized for its present needs. Alternate reasons for restructing include a change of ownership or ownership structure, demerger repositioning debt _____ and financial _____.

a. Concentrated stock
b. Day trading
c. Cross-border leasing
d. Restructuring

56. In finance, the _____ approach describes a method of valuing a project, company, or asset using the concepts of the time value of money. All future cash flows are estimated and discounted to give their present values. The discount rate used is generally the appropriate cost of capital and may incorporate judgments of the uncertainty (riskiness) of the future cash flows.

a. Future-oriented
b. Net present value
c. Present value of benefits
d. Discounted cash flow

57. In economics, _____ is a rise in the general level of prices of goods and services in an economy over a period of time. The term '_____' once referred to increases in the money supply (monetary _____); however, economic debates about the relationship between money supply and price levels have led to its primary use today in describing price _____. _____ can also be described as a decline in the real value of money--a loss of purchasing power in the medium of exchange which is also the monetary unit of account.

a. ABN Amro
b. A Random Walk Down Wall Street
c. AAB
d. Inflation

58. _____ in business is an accounting concept that refers to ownership of a company (subsidiary) that is less than 50% of outstanding shares. _____ belongs to other investors and is reported on the consolidated balance sheet of the owning company to reflect the claim on assets belonging to other, non-controlling shareholders. Also, _____ is reported on the consolidated income statement as a share of profit belonging to minority shareholders.

a. Fixed asset
b. Construction in Progress
c. Credit memo
d. Minority interest

59. _____ is a valuation model that assumes the stock market sets prices based on cash flow, not on corporate performance and earnings.

_____ = Cash Flow / Market Recapitalization

For the corporation, it is essentially internal rate of return (IRR.) _____ is compared to a hurdle rate to determine if investment/product is performing adequately.

a. Regulation FD
b. Revenue recognition
c. Regulation Fair Disclosure
d. Cash flow return on investment

60. In finance, _____, also known as return on investment is the ratio of money gained or lost on an investment relative to the amount of money invested. The amount of money gained or lost may be referred to as interest, profit/loss, gain/loss, or net income/loss. The money invested may be referred to as the asset, capital, principal, or the cost basis of the investment.

Chapter 7. Analyzing Historical Performance

a. Rate of return
c. Composiition of Creditors
b. Doctrine of the Proper Law
d. Stock or scrip dividends

61. _____ is an accounting term used to reflect the portion of the book value of a business entity not directly attributable to its assets and liabilities; it normally arises only in case of an acquisition. It reflects the ability of the entity to make a higher profit than would be derived from selling the tangible assets. _____ is also known as an intangible asset.
a. Cost of goods sold
b. Consolidation
c. Net profit
d. Goodwill

62. _____ means a rise of a price of goods or products. This term is specially used as _____ of a currency, where it means a rise of currency to the relation with a foreign currency in a fixed exchange rate. In floating exchange rate correct term would be appreciation.
a. Correlation trading
b. Revaluation
c. Common pool problem
d. Holding period return

63. The _____ is a financial term defined as a company's operating expenses as a percentage of revenue. This financial ratio is most commonly used for industries such as railroads which require a large percentage of revenues to maintain operations. In railroading, an _____ of 80 or lower is considered desirable.
a. Internal financing
b. Underwriting contract
c. Employee stock option
d. Operating ratio

64. A _____ is a private or public market for the trading of company stock and derivatives of company stock at an agreed price; these are securities listed on a stock exchange as well as those only traded privately.

The size of the world _____ is estimated at about $36.6 trillion US at the beginning of October 2008 . The world derivatives market has been estimated at about $480 trillion face or nominal value, 12 times the size of the entire world economy.

a. Adolph Coors
b. Andrew Tobias
c. Anton Gelonkin
d. Stock market

Chapter 8. Forecasting Performance

1. In financial accounting, a _____ or statement of financial position is a summary of a person's or organization's balances. Assets, liabilities and ownership equity are listed as of a specific date, such as the end of its financial year. A _____ is often described as a snapshot of a company's financial condition.

   a. Statement on Auditing Standards No. 70: Service Organizations
   b. Balance sheet
   c. Statement of retained earnings
   d. Financial statements

2. _____ are formal records of a business' financial activities.

   _____ provide an overview of a business' financial condition in both short and long term. There are four basic _____:

   1. **Balance sheet**: also referred to as statement of financial position or condition, reports on a company's assets, liabilities, and net equity as of a given point in time.
   2. **Income statement**: also referred to as Profit and Loss statement (or a 'P'L'), reports on a company's income, expenses, and profits over a period of time.
   3. **Statement of retained earnings**: explains the changes in a company's retained earnings over the reporting period.
   4. **Statement of cash flows**: reports on a company's cash flow activities, particularly its operating, investing and financing activities.

   a. Statement of retained earnings
   b. Statement on Auditing Standards No. 70: Service Organizations
   c. Financial statements
   d. Notes to the Financial Statements

3. _____, refers to consumption opportunity gained by an entity within a specified time frame, which is generally expressed in monetary terms. However, for households and individuals, '_____ is the sum of all the wages, salaries, profits, interests payments, rents and other forms of earnings received... in a given period of time.' For firms, _____ generally refers to net-profit: what remains of revenue after expenses have been subtracted.

   a. Income
   b. Accrual
   c. Annual report
   d. OIBDA

4. An _____ is a financial statement for companies that indicates how Revenue is transformed into net income The purpose of the _____ is to show managers and investors whether the company made or lost money during the period being reported.

   The important thing to remember about an _____ is that it represents a period of time.

   a. ABN Amro
   b. AAB
   c. A Random Walk Down Wall Street
   d. Income statement

Chapter 8. Forecasting Performance

5. _____ is the balance of the amounts of cash being received and paid by a business during a defined period of time, sometimes tied to a specific project. Measurement of _____ can be used

- to evaluate the state or performance of a business or project.
- to determine problems with liquidity. Being profitable does not necessarily mean being liquid. A company can fail because of a shortage of cash, even while profitable.
- to generate project rate of returns. The time of _____s into and out of projects are used as inputs to financial models such as internal rate of return, and net present value.
- to examine income or growth of a business when it is believed that accrual accounting concepts do not represent economic realities. Alternately, _____ can be used to 'validate' the net income generated by accrual accounting.

_____ as a generic term may be used differently depending on context, and certain _____ definitions may be adapted by analysts and users for their own uses. Common terms include operating _____ and free _____.

_____s can be classified into:

1. Operational _____s: Cash received or expended as a result of the company's core business activities.
2. Investment _____s: Cash received or expended through capital expenditure, investments or acquisitions.
3. Financing _____s: Cash received or expended as a result of financial activities, such as interests and dividends.

All three together - the net _____ - are necessary to reconcile the beginning cash balance to the ending cash balance. Loan draw downs or equity injections, that is just shifting of capital but no expenditure as such, are not considered in the net _____.

a. Cash flow
b. Real option
c. Shareholder value
d. Corporate finance

6. In corporate finance, _____ is a cash flow available for distribution among all the security holders of a company. They include equity holders, debt holders, preferred stock holders, convertible security holders, and so on.

Note that the first three lines above are calculated for you on the standard Statement of Cash Flows.

a. Funding
b. Safety stock
c. Forfaiting
d. Free cash flow

7. _____ is a financial measure that quantifies how well a company generates cash flow relative to the capital it has invested in its business. It is defined as Net operating profit less adjusted taxes divided by Invested Capital and is usually expressed as a percentage. In this calculation, capital invested includes all monetary capital invested: long-term debt, common and preferred shares.

a. Return on invested capital
b. Sharpe ratio
c. Debt service coverage ratio
d. Cash conversion cycle

Chapter 8. Forecasting Performance

8. In business and accounting, _____s are everything of value that is owned by a person or company. The balance sheet of a firm records the monetary value of the _____s owned by the firm. The two major _____ classes are tangible _____s and intangible _____s.

   a. Income
   b. EBITDA
   c. Asset
   d. Accounts payable

9. _____ represents the total cash investment that shareholders and debtholders have made in a company. There are two different but completely equivalent methods for calculating _____. The operating approach is calculated as:

   _____ = Operating Net Working Capital + Net PP'E + Capitalized Operating Leases + Other Operating Assets + Operating Intangibles - Other Operating Liabilities - Cumulative Adjustment for Amortization of R'D

   Equivalently, the financing approach is calculated as:

   In symbols:

   $$K = D + E - M$$

   _____ is used in several important measurements of financial performance, including return on _____, economic value added, and free cash flow.

   a. Operating leverage
   b. Information ratio
   c. Invested capital
   d. Inventory turnover

10. In business, _____ is income that a company receives from its normal business activities, usually from the sale of goods and services to customers. Some companies also receive _____ from interest, dividends or royalties paid to them by other companies. _____ may refer to business income in general, or it may refer to the amount, in a monetary unit, received during a period of time, as in 'Last year, Company X had _____ of $32 million.'

   In many countries, including the UK, _____ is referred to as turnover.

   a. Bottom line
   b. Matching principle
   c. Furniture, Fixtures and Equipment
   d. Revenue

11. The American Oil Company founded in Baltimore in 1910 and incorporated in 1922 by Louis Blaustein and his son Jacob, but is now part of BP. The firm's early innovations include the gasoline tanker truck and the drive-through filling station.

   In 1923 the Blausteins sold a half interest in _____ to the Pan American Petroleum ' Transport company in exchange for a guaranteed supply of oil.

   a. ABN Amro
   b. AAB
   c. A Random Walk Down Wall Street
   d. Amoco

12. _____ methods are means of managing inventory and financial matters involving the money a company ties up within inventory of produced goods, raw materials, parts, components, or feed stocks.

In LIFO accounting, a historical method of recording the value of inventory, a firm records the last units purchased as the first units sold. LIFO is an acronym for 'last in, first out.' Sometimes the term FILO ('first in, last out') is used synonymously.

 a. General journal
 b. Net sales
 c. FIFO and LIFO accounting
 d. Payroll

13. _____ is a term used in accounting, economics and finance to spread the cost of an asset over the span of several years.

In simple words we can say that _____ is the reduction in the value of an asset due to usage, passage of time, wear and tear, technological outdating or obsolescence, depletion or other such factors.

In accounting, _____ is a term used to describe any method of attributing the historical or purchase cost of an asset across its useful life, roughly corresponding to normal wear and tear.

 a. Bottom line
 b. Deferred financing costs
 c. Matching principle
 d. Depreciation

14. An _____, operating expenditure, operational expense, operational expenditure or OPEX is an on-going cost for running a product, business, or system. Its counterpart, a capital expenditure (CAPEX), is the cost of developing or providing non-consumable parts for the product or system. For example, the purchase of a photocopier is the CAPEX, and the annual paper and toner cost is the OPEX.
 a. A Random Walk Down Wall Street
 b. AAB
 c. ABN Amro
 d. Operating expense

15. _____ is a fee paid on borrowed assets. It is the price paid for the use of borrowed money , or, money earned by deposited funds . Assets that are sometimes lent with _____ include money, shares, consumer goods through hire purchase, major assets such as aircraft, and even entire factories in finance lease arrangements.
 a. Insolvency
 b. Interest
 c. AAB
 d. A Random Walk Down Wall Street

16. In finance, _____ refers to the way a corporation finances its assets through some combination of equity, debt, or hybrid securities. A firm's _____ is then the composition or 'structure' of its liabilities. For example, a firm that sells $20 billion in equity and $80 billion in debt is said to be 20% equity-financed and 80% debt-financed.
 a. Market for corporate control
 b. Capital structure
 c. Book building
 d. Rights issue

17. _____ is a financial metric which represents operating liquidity available to a business. Along with fixed assets such as plant and equipment, _____ is considered a part of operating capital. It is calculated as current assets minus current liabilities.
 a. 4-4-5 Calendar
 b. Working capital management
 c. 529 plan
 d. Working capital

18. _____ is an accounting term used to reflect the portion of the book value of a business entity not directly attributable to its assets and liabilities; it normally arises only in case of an acquisition. It reflects the ability of the entity to make a higher profit than would be derived from selling the tangible assets. _____ is also known as an intangible asset.
   a. Goodwill
   b. Cost of goods sold
   c. Consolidation
   d. Net profit

19. _____ is the process of decreasing an amount over a period of time. The word comes from Middle English amortisen to kill, alienate in mortmain, from Anglo-French amorteser, alteration of amortir, from Vulgar Latin admortire to kill, from Latin ad- + mort-, mors death. Particular instances of the term include:

   - _____ (business), the allocation of a lump sum amount to different time periods, particularly for loans and other forms of finance, including related interest or other finance charges.
     - _____ schedule, a table detailing each periodic payment on a loan (typically a mortgage), as generated by an _____ calculator.
     - Negative _____, an _____ schedule where the loan amount actually increases through not paying the full interest
   - Amortized analysis, analyzing the execution cost of algorithms over a sequence of operations.
   - _____ of capital expenditures of certain assets under accounting rules, particularly intangible assets, in a manner analogous to depreciation.
   - _____ (tax law)

_____ is also used in the context of zoning regulations and describes the time in which a property owner has to relocate when the property's use constitutes a preexisting nonconforming use under zoning regulations.

   - Depreciation

   a. Amortization
   b. AT'T Inc.
   c. Intrinsic value
   d. Option

20. _____ or financing is to provide capital (funds), which means money for a project, a person, a business or any other private or public institutions.

Those funds can be allocated for either short term or long term purposes. The health fund is a new way of _____ private healthcare centers.

   a. Funding
   b. Product life cycle
   c. Proxy fight
   d. Synthetic CDO

21. In finance, _____ is the process of estimating the potential market value of a financial asset or liability. they can be done on assets (for example, investments in marketable securities such as stocks, options, business enterprises, or intangible assets such as patents and trademarks) or on liabilities (e.g., Bonds issued by a company.) _____ s are required in many contexts including investment analysis, capital budgeting, merger and acquisition transactions, financial reporting, taxable events to determine the proper tax liability, and in litigation.

a. Valuation
b. Procter ' Gamble
c. Margin
d. Share

22. In economics, business, and accounting, a _____ is the value of money that has been used up to produce something, and hence is not available for use anymore. In business, the _____ may be one of acquisition, in which case the amount of money expended to acquire it is counted as _____. In this case, money is the input that is gone in order to acquire the thing.
  a. Sliding scale fees
  b. Fixed costs
  c. Marginal cost
  d. Cost

23. _____ are expenses that change in proportion to the activity of a business. In other words, _____ are the sum of marginal costs. It can also be considered normal costs. Along with fixed costs, _____ make up the two components of total cost. Direct Costs, however, are costs that can be associated with a particular cost object.
  a. Transaction cost
  b. Fixed costs
  c. Cost accounting
  d. Variable costs

24. In economics, _____ is a rise in the general level of prices of goods and services in an economy over a period of time. The term '_____' once referred to increases in the money supply (monetary _____); however, economic debates about the relationship between money supply and price levels have led to its primary use today in describing price _____. _____ can also be described as a decline in the real value of money--a loss of purchasing power in the medium of exchange which is also the monetary unit of account.
  a. AAB
  b. ABN Amro
  c. A Random Walk Down Wall Street
  d. Inflation

25. In finance, a _____ is a debt security, in which the authorized issuer owes the holders a debt and, depending on the terms of the _____, is obliged to pay interest (the coupon) and/or to repay the principal at a later date, termed maturity.

Thus a _____ is a loan: the issuer is the borrower, the _____ holder is the lender, and the coupon is the interest. _____s provide the borrower with external funds to finance long-term investments, or, in the case of government _____s, to finance current expenditure.

  a. Puttable bond
  b. Convertible bond
  c. Catastrophe bonds
  d. Bond

26. A _____ is a measure of the average price of consumer goods and services purchased by households. The _____ can be used to index (i.e., adjust for the effects of inflation) wages, salaries, pensions, or regulated or contracted prices. The _____ is, along with the population census and the National Income and Product Accounts, one of the most closely watched national economic statistics.
  a. 529 plan
  b. Divisia index
  c. 4-4-5 Calendar
  d. Consumer price index

27. _____ are bonds where the principal is indexed to inflation. They are thus designed to cut out the inflation risk of an investment. _____ pay a periodic coupon that is equal to the product of the inflation index and the nominal coupon rate. The relationship between coupon payments, breakeven inflation and real interest rates is given by the Fisher equation.

Chapter 8. Forecasting Performance

a. A Random Walk Down Wall Street
b. ABN Amro
c. Inflation-indexed bonds
d. AAB

28. A _____ is a normalized average (typically a weighted average) of prices for a given class of goods or services in a given region, during a given interval of time. It is a statistic designed to help to compare how these prices, taken as a whole, differ between time periods or geographical locations.
   a. Discounts and allowances
   b. Price discrimination
   c. Transfer pricing
   d. Price index

29. _____ in business is an accounting concept that refers to ownership of a company (subsidiary) that is less than 50% of outstanding shares. _____ belongs to other investors and is reported on the consolidated balance sheet of the owning company to reflect the claim on assets belonging to other, non-controlling shareholders. Also, _____ is reported on the consolidated income statement as a share of profit belonging to minority shareholders.
   a. Fixed asset
   b. Construction in Progress
   c. Credit memo
   d. Minority interest

30. _____ plant, and equipment, is a term used in accountancy for assets and property which cannot easily be converted into cash. This can be compared with current assets such as cash or bank accounts, which are described as liquid assets. In most cases, only tangible assets are referred to as fixed.
   a. Percentage of Completion
   b. Remittance advice
   c. Petty cash
   d. Fixed asset

31. In financial accounting, _____s are precautions for which the amount or probability of occurrence are not known. Typical examples are _____s for warranty costs and _____ for taxes the term reserve is used instead of term _____; such a use, however, is inconsistent with the terminology suggested by International Accounting Standards Board.
   a. Petty cash
   b. Momentum Accounting and Triple-Entry Bookkeeping
   c. Money measurement concept
   d. Provision

32. _____, in accrual accounting, is any account where the asset or liability is not realized until a future date, e.g. annuities, charges, taxes, income, etc. The _____ item may be carried, dependent on type of deferral, as either an asset or liability. See also: accrual

_____ is also used in the university admissions process. It is the action by which a school rejects a student for early admission but still opts to review that student in the general admissions pool.

   a. Revenue
   b. Net profit
   c. Current asset
   d. Deferred

33. _____ is an accounting concept, meaning a future tax liability or asset, resulting from temporary differences between book (accounting) value of assets and liabilities and their tax value, or timing differences between the recognition of gains and losses in financial statements and their recognition in a tax computation.

Temporary differences are differences between the carrying amount of an asset or liability recognised in the balance sheet and the amount attributed to that asset or liability for tax purposes (the tax base.)

Temporary differences may be either:

- taxable temporary differences, which are temporary differences that will result in taxable amounts in determining taxable profit (tax loss) of future periods when the carrying amount of the asset or liability is recovered or settled; or
- deductible temporary differences, which are temporary differences that will result in deductible amounts in determining taxable profit (tax loss) of future periods when the carrying amount of the asset or liability is recovered or settled.

The tax base of an asset or liability is the amount attributed to that asset or liability for tax purposes:

- the tax base of an asset is the amount that will be deductible for tax purposes against any taxable economic benefits that will flow to an entity when it recovers the carrying amount of the asset.

- the tax base of a liability is its carrying amount, less any amount that will be deductible for tax purposes in respect of that liability in future periods.

The basic principle of accounting for _____ under a temporary difference approach can be illustrated using a common example in which a company has fixed assets which qualify for tax depreciation.

a. Deferred Tax
b. Qualified residence interest
c. Tax exemption
d. Monetary policy

34. The _____ is a financial term defined as a company's operating expenses as a percentage of revenue. This financial ratio is most commonly used for industries such as railroads which require a large percentage of revenues to maintain operations. In railroading, an _____ of 80 or lower is considered desirable.

a. Operating ratio
b. Employee stock option
c. Underwriting contract
d. Internal financing

Chapter 9. Estimating Continuing Value

1. _____ = net operating profit less adjusted taxes.

Used in preference to Net Income as it removes the effects of capital structure (debt vs. equity.) The Operating Profit is prior to interest and taxes being subtracted, which makes _____ equal NOPAT.

a. Consolidated financial statements
b. NOPLAT
c. Coupon leverage
d. Flight-to-quality

2. _____ represents the total cash investment that shareholders and debtholders have made in a company. There are two different but completely equivalent methods for calculating _____. The operating approach is calculated as:

_____ = Operating Net Working Capital + Net PP'E + Capitalized Operating Leases + Other Operating Assets + Operating Intangibles - Other Operating Liabilities - Cumulative Adjustment for Amortization of R'D

Equivalently, the financing approach is calculated as:

In symbols:

$$K = D + E - M$$

_____ is used in several important measurements of financial performance, including return on _____, economic value added, and free cash flow.

a. Invested capital
b. Information ratio
c. Operating leverage
d. Inventory turnover

3. _____ is a measure of a company's earning power from ongoing operations, equal to earnings before the deduction of interest payments and income taxes.

To accountants, economic profit, or EP, is a single-period metric to determine the value created by a company in one period - usually a year. It is the net profit after tax less the equity charge, a risk-weighted cost of capital.

a. Economic profit
b. A Random Walk Down Wall Street
c. AAB
d. Operating profit

4. _____ is the difference between price and the costs of bringing to market whatever it is that is accounted as an enterprise (whether by harvest, extraction, manufacture, or purchase) in terms of the component costs of delivered goods and/or services and any operating or other expenses.

A key difficulty in measuring profit is in defining costs. Pure economic monetary profits can be zero or negative even in competitive equilibrium when accounted monetized costs exceed monetized price.

a. Accounting profit
b. Economic profit
c. A Random Walk Down Wall Street
d. AAB

Chapter 9. Estimating Continuing Value

5. In finance, _____, also known as return on investment is the ratio of money gained or lost on an investment relative to the amount of money invested. The amount of money gained or lost may be referred to as interest, profit/loss, gain/loss, or net income/loss. The money invested may be referred to as the asset, capital, principal, or the cost basis of the investment.
   a. Stock or scrip dividends
   b. Composiition of Creditors
   c. Rate of return
   d. Doctrine of the Proper Law

6. Pure _____ is the increase in wealth that an investor has from making an investment, taking into consideration all costs associated with that investment including the opportunity cost of capital.

A key difficulty in measuring profit is in defining costs. Pure economic monetary profits can be zero or negative even in competitive equilibrium when accounted monetized costs exceed monetized price.

   a. AAB
   b. Economic profit
   c. Operating profit
   d. A Random Walk Down Wall Street

7. In finance, _____ is the process of estimating the potential market value of a financial asset or liability. they can be done on assets (for example, investments in marketable securities such as stocks, options, business enterprises, or intangible assets such as patents and trademarks) or on liabilities (e.g., Bonds issued by a company.) _____s are required in many contexts including investment analysis, capital budgeting, merger and acquisition transactions, financial reporting, taxable events to determine the proper tax liability, and in litigation.
   a. Margin
   b. Valuation
   c. Procter ' Gamble
   d. Share

8. _____ is the balance of the amounts of cash being received and paid by a business during a defined period of time, sometimes tied to a specific project. Measurement of _____ can be used

   - to evaluate the state or performance of a business or project.
   - to determine problems with liquidity. Being profitable does not necessarily mean being liquid. A company can fail because of a shortage of cash, even while profitable.
   - to generate project rate of returns. The time of _____s into and out of projects are used as inputs to financial models such as internal rate of return, and net present value.
   - to examine income or growth of a business when it is believed that accrual accounting concepts do not represent economic realities. Alternately, _____ can be used to 'validate' the net income generated by accrual accounting.

_____ as a generic term may be used differently depending on context, and certain _____ definitions may be adapted by analysts and users for their own uses. Common terms include operating _____ and free _____.

_____s can be classified into:

1. Operational _____s: Cash received or expended as a result of the company's core business activities.
2. Investment _____s: Cash received or expended through capital expenditure, investments or acquisitions.
3. Financing _____s: Cash received or expended as a result of financial activities, such as interests and dividends.

Chapter 9. Estimating Continuing Value

All three together - the net _____ - are necessary to reconcile the beginning cash balance to the ending cash balance. Loan draw downs or equity injections, that is just shifting of capital but no expenditure as such, are not considered in the net _____.

a. Cash flow
c. Shareholder value
b. Corporate finance
d. Real option

9. In finance, the _____ approach describes a method of valuing a project, company, or asset using the concepts of the time value of money. All future cash flows are estimated and discounted to give their present values. The discount rate used is generally the appropriate cost of capital and may incorporate judgments of the uncertainty (riskiness) of the future cash flows.

a. Future-oriented
c. Discounted cash flow
b. Present value of benefits
d. Net present value

10. In law, _____ refers to the process by which a company (or part of a company) is brought to an end, and the assets and property of the company redistributed. _____ can also be referred to as winding-up or dissolution, although dissolution technically refers to the last stage of _____. The process of _____ also arises when customs, an authority or agency in a country responsible for collecting and safeguarding customs duties, determines the final computation or ascertainment of the duties or drawback accruing on an entry.

a. Debt settlement
c. Liquidation
b. 4-4-5 Calendar
d. 529 plan

11. _____ is the likely price of an asset when it is allowed insufficient time to sell on the open market, thereby reducing its exposure to potential buyers. _____ is typically lower than fair market value. Unlike cash or securities, certain illiquid assets, like real estate, often require a period of several months in order to obtain their fair market value in a sale, and will generally sell for a significantly lower price if a sale is forced to occur in a shorter time period.

a. Tenancy
c. REIT
b. Real estate investing
d. Liquidation value

12. The term _____ or replacement value refers to the amount that an entity would have to pay, at the present time, to replace any one of its assets.

In the insurance industry, '_____' is a method of computing the value of an item insured. _____ is not market value, but is instead the cost to replace an item or structure at its pre-loss condition.

a. Bonus share
c. January effect
b. False billing
d. Replacement cost

13. In economics, business, and accounting, a _____ is the value of money that has been used up to produce something, and hence is not available for use anymore. In business, the _____ may be one of acquisition, in which case the amount of money expended to acquire it is counted as _____. In this case, money is the input that is gone in order to acquire the thing.

a. Fixed costs
c. Sliding scale fees
b. Cost
d. Marginal cost

Chapter 10. Estimating the Cost of Capital

1. In economics, business, and accounting, a _____ is the value of money that has been used up to produce something, and hence is not available for use anymore. In business, the _____ may be one of acquisition, in which case the amount of money expended to acquire it is counted as _____. In this case, money is the input that is gone in order to acquire the thing.

   a. Cost
   b. Fixed costs
   c. Marginal cost
   d. Sliding scale fees

2. The _____ is an expected return that the provider of capital plans to earn on their investment.

   Capital (money) used for funding a business should earn returns for the capital providers who risk their capital. For an investment to be worthwhile, the expected return on capital must be greater than the _____.

   a. Capital intensity
   b. Weighted average cost of capital
   c. Cost of capital
   d. 4-4-5 Calendar

3. The _____ is the rate that a company is expected to pay to finance its assets. WACC is the minimum return that a company must earn on existing asset base to satisfy its creditors, owners, and other providers of capital.

   Companies raise money from a number of sources: common equity, preferred equity, straight debt, convertible debt, exchangeable debt, warrants, options, pension liabilities, executive stock options, governmental subsidies, and so on.

   a. Cost of capital
   b. 4-4-5 Calendar
   c. Capital intensity
   d. Weighted average cost of capital

4. _____ is the balance of the amounts of cash being received and paid by a business during a defined period of time, sometimes tied to a specific project. Measurement of _____ can be used

   - to evaluate the state or performance of a business or project.
   - to determine problems with liquidity. Being profitable does not necessarily mean being liquid. A company can fail because of a shortage of cash, even while profitable.
   - to generate project rate of returns. The time of _____s into and out of projects are used as inputs to financial models such as internal rate of return, and net present value.
   - to examine income or growth of a business when it is believed that accrual accounting concepts do not represent economic realities. Alternately, _____ can be used to 'validate' the net income generated by accrual accounting.

   _____ as a generic term may be used differently depending on context, and certain _____ definitions may be adapted by analysts and users for their own uses. Common terms include operating _____ and free _____.

Chapter 10. Estimating the Cost of Capital

_____s can be classified into:

1. Operational _____s: Cash received or expended as a result of the company's core business activities.
2. Investment _____s: Cash received or expended through capital expenditure, investments or acquisitions.
3. Financing _____s: Cash received or expended as a result of financial activities, such as interests and dividends.

All three together - the net _____ - are necessary to reconcile the beginning cash balance to the ending cash balance. Loan draw downs or equity injections, that is just shifting of capital but no expenditure as such, are not considered in the net _____.

a. Cash flow
b. Shareholder value
c. Real option
d. Corporate finance

5. In corporate finance, _____ is a cash flow available for distribution among all the security holders of a company. They include equity holders, debt holders, preferred stock holders, convertible security holders, and so on.

Note that the first three lines above are calculated for you on the standard Statement of Cash Flows.

a. Safety stock
b. Funding
c. Forfaiting
d. Free cash flow

6. The term _____ has three unrelated technical definitions, and is also used in a variety of non-technical ways.

- In financial economics, it refers to any asset used to make money, as opposed to assets used for personal enjoyment or consumption. This is an important distinction because two people can disagree sharply about the value of personal assets, one person might think a sports car is more valuable than a pickup truck, another person might have the opposite taste. But if an asset is held for the purpose of making money, taste has nothing to do with it, only differences of opinion about how much money the asset will produce. With the further assumption that people agree on the probability distribution of future cash flows, it is possible to have an objective _____ pricing model. Even without the assumption of agreement, it is possible to set rational limits on _____ value.
- In governmental accounting, it is defined as any asset used in operations with an initial useful life extending beyond one reporting period. Generally, government managers have a 'stewardship' duty to maintain _____s under their control. See International Public Sector Accounting Standards for details.
- In US tax accounting, it is defined as any property other than a list of exceptions. The main exceptions are anything held for sale, and any real estate or depreciable property used in business. Almost everything you own and use for personal purposes, pleasure or investment is a _____. If something is a _____ for tax purposes, gains or losses on sale or disposition are capital gains or capital losses. For individuals, however, capital losses on property held for personal use are generally not deductible. See the IRS publication Tax Facts about Capital Gains and Losses for details.

A well-known financial accounting textbook advises that the term be avoided except in tax accounting because it is used in so many different senses, not all of them well-defined. For example it is often used as a synonym for fixed assets or for investments in securities.

Chapter 10. Estimating the Cost of Capital 53

A common non-technical usage occurs when people ask that employees or the environment or something else be treated as a _____.

a. Solvency
c. Capital asset
b. Political risk
d. Settlement date

7. In finance, the _____ is used to determine a theoretically appropriate required rate of return of an asset, if that asset is to be added to an already well-diversified portfolio, given that asset's non-diversifiable risk. The model takes into account the asset's sensitivity to non-diversifiable risk (also known as systemic risk or market risk), often represented by the quantity beta (β) in the financial industry, as well as the expected return of the market and the expected return of a theoretical risk-free asset.

The model was introduced by Jack Treynor (1961, 1962), William Sharpe (1964), John Lintner (1965a,b) and Jan Mossin (1966) independently, building on the earlier work of Harry Markowitz on diversification and modern portfolio theory.

a. Cox-Ingersoll-Ross model
c. Random walk hypothesis
b. Hull-White model
d. Capital asset pricing model

8. In business and accounting, _____ s are everything of value that is owned by a person or company. The balance sheet of a firm records the monetary value of the _____ s owned by the firm. The two major _____ classes are tangible _____ s and intangible _____ s.
a. EBITDA
c. Asset
b. Income
d. Accounts payable

9. In finance, _____ is the process of estimating the potential market value of a financial asset or liability. they can be done on assets (for example, investments in marketable securities such as stocks, options, business enterprises, or intangible assets such as patents and trademarks) or on liabilities (e.g., Bonds issued by a company.) _____ s are required in many contexts including investment analysis, capital budgeting, merger and acquisition transactions, financial reporting, taxable events to determine the proper tax liability, and in litigation.
a. Margin
c. Procter ' Gamble
b. Share
d. Valuation

10. In finance, the _____ is the minimum rate of return a firm must offer shareholders to compensate for waiting for their returns, and for bearing some risk.

The _____ capital for a particular company is the rate of return on investment that is required by the company's ordinary shareholders. The return consists both of dividend and capital gains, e.g. increases in the share price.

a. Round-tripping
c. Net pay
b. Cost of equity
d. Residual value

Chapter 10. Estimating the Cost of Capital

11. A _____ is an international bond that is denominated in a currency not native to the country where it is issued. It can be categorised according to the currency in which it is issued. London is one of the centers of the _____ market, but _____s may be traded throughout the world - for example in Singapore or Tokyo.

   a. Eurobond
   b. Economic entity
   c. Education production function
   d. Interest rate option

12. A _____ is a bond issued by a national government denominated in the country's own currency. Bonds issued by national governments in foreign currencies are normally referred to as sovereign bonds. The first ever _____ was issued by the British government in 1693 to raise money to fund a war against France.

   a. Collateralized debt obligations
   b. Zero-coupon bond
   c. Municipal bond
   d. Government bond

13. In finance, a _____ is a debt security, in which the authorized issuer owes the holders a debt and, depending on the terms of the _____, is obliged to pay interest (the coupon) and/or to repay the principal at a later date, termed maturity.

   Thus a _____ is a loan: the issuer is the borrower, the _____ holder is the lender, and the coupon is the interest. _____s provide the borrower with external funds to finance long-term investments, or, in the case of government _____s, to finance current expenditure.

   a. Puttable bond
   b. Convertible bond
   c. Bond
   d. Catastrophe bonds

14. _____ is the risk that the value of an investment will decrease due to moves in market factors. The five standard _____ factors are:

   - Equity risk, the risk that stock prices will change.
   - Interest rate risk, the risk that interest rates will change.
   - Currency risk, the risk that foreign exchange rates will change.
   - Commodity risk, the risk that commodity prices (e.g. grains, metals) will change.

   As with other forms of risk, _____ may be measured in a number of ways. Traditionally, this is done using a Value at Risk methodology. Value at risk is well established as a risk management technique, but it contains a number of limiting assumptions that constrain its accuracy.

   a. Transaction risk
   b. Tracking error
   c. Market risk
   d. Currency risk

15.

   In finance, the _____ can be the expected rate of return above the risk-free interest rate. When measuring risk, a common sense approach is to compare the risk-free return on T-bills and the very risky return on other investments. The difference between these two returns can be interpreted as a measure of the excess return on the average risky asset. This excess return is known as the _____.

Chapter 10. Estimating the Cost of Capital

a. Risk modeling
c. Risk aversion
b. Risk adjusted return on capital
d. Risk premium

16. In finance, the term _____ describes the amount in cash that returns to the owners of a security. Normally it does not include the price variations, at the difference of the total return. _____ applies to various stated rates of return on stocks (common and preferred, and convertible), fixed income instruments (bonds, notes, bills, strips, zero coupon), and some other investment type insurance products (e.g. annuities.)

a. Yield
c. Macaulay duration
b. 4-4-5 Calendar
d. Yield to maturity

17. _____ is a mathematical tool for finding repeating patterns, such as the presence of a periodic signal which has been buried under noise, or identifying the missing fundamental frequency in a signal implied by its harmonic frequencies. It is used frequently in signal processing for analyzing functions or series of values, such as time domain signals. Informally, it is the similarity between observations as a function of the time separation between them.

a. ABN Amro
c. A Random Walk Down Wall Street
b. AAB
d. Autocorrelation

18. In finance, _____ is the tendency for failed companies to be excluded from performance studies because they no longer exist. It often causes the results of studies to skew higher because only companies which were successful enough to survive until the end of the period are included.

For example, a mutual fund company's selection of funds today will include only those that have been successful in the past.

a. 7-Eleven
c. 4-4-5 Calendar
b. 529 plan
d. Survivorship bias

19. The _____ is a United States government system for classifying industries by a four-digit code. Established in 1937, it is being supplanted by the six-digit North American Industry Classification System, which was released in 1997; however certain government departments and agencies, such as the U.S. Securities and Exchange Commission (SEC), still use the _____ codes.

The following table is from the SEC's site, which allows searching for companies by _____ code in its database of filings.

a. 4-4-5 Calendar
c. Standard Industrial Classification
b. 529 plan
d. 7-Eleven

20. In the portfolio management field, Eugene Fama and Kenneth French developed the highly successful _____ to describe market behavior.

CAPM uses a single factor, beta, to compare the excess returns of a portfolio with the excess returns of the market as a whole. But it oversimplifies the complex market. Fama and French started with the observation that two classes of stocks have tended to do better than the market as a whole: small caps and (ii) stocks with a high book-to-market ratio (BM, customarily called value stocks, and different from growth stocks). They then added two factors to CAPM to reflect a portfolio's exposure to these two classes:

Chapter 10. Estimating the Cost of Capital

Here r is the portfolio's return rate, R_f is the risk-free return rate, and K_m is the return of the whole stock market. The 'three factor' >β is analogous to the classical >β but not equal to it, since there are now two additional factors to do some of the work. SMB stands for 'small minus big' and HML for 'high (book-to-price ratio) minus low'; they measure the historic excess returns of small caps over big caps and of value stocks over growth stocks.

a. Fama-French three factor model
b. Reputational risk
c. Guaranteed investment contracts
d. Mitigating Control

21. A _____ is a portfolio consisting of a weighted sum of every asset in the market, with weights in the proportions that they exist in the market (with the necessary assumption that these assets are infinitely divisible.)

Neha Tyagi's critique (1977) states that this is only a theoretical concept, as to create a _____ for investment purposes in practice would necessarily include every single possible available asset, including real estate, precious metals, stamp collections, jewelry, and anything with any worth, as the theoretical market being referred to would be the world market. As a result, proxies for the market are used in practice by investors.

a. Market portfolio
b. Central Securities Depository
c. Delta neutral
d. Market price

22. In statistics and image processing, to smooth a data set is to create an approximating function that attempts to capture important patterns in the data, while leaving out noise or other fine-scale structures/rapid phenomena. Many different algorithms are used in _____. One of the most common algorithms is the 'moving average', often used to try to capture important trends in repeated statistical surveys.
a. 4-4-5 Calendar
b. 529 plan
c. 7-Eleven
d. Smoothing

23. In economics and finance, _____ is the practice of taking advantage of a price differential between two or more markets: striking a combination of matching deals that capitalize upon the imbalance, the profit being the difference between the market prices. When used by academics, an _____ is a transaction that involves no negative cash flow at any probabilistic or temporal state and a positive cash flow in at least one state; in simple terms, a risk-free profit.
a. Issuer
b. Arbitrage
c. Initial margin
d. Efficient-market hypothesis

24. _____ , in finance, is a general theory of asset pricing, that has become influential in the pricing of stocks.

_____ holds that the expected return of a financial asset can be modeled as a linear function of various macro-economic factors or theoretical market indices, where sensitivity to changes in each factor is represented by a factor-specific beta coefficient. The model-derived rate of return will then be used to price the asset correctly - the asset price should equal the expected end of period price discounted at the rate implied by model.

a. AAB
b. ABN Amro
c. A Random Walk Down Wall Street
d. Arbitrage pricing theory

25. _____ is that which is owed; usually referencing assets owed, but the term can cover other obligations. In the case of assets, _____ is a means of using future purchasing power in the present before a summation has been earned. Some companies and corporations use _____ as a part of their overall corporate finance strategy.
   a. Partial Payment
   b. Cross-collateralization
   c. Credit cycle
   d. Debt

26. In finance, _____ refers to the way a corporation finances its assets through some combination of equity, debt, or hybrid securities. A firm's _____ is then the composition or 'structure' of its liabilities. For example, a firm that sells $20 billion in equity and $80 billion in debt is said to be 20% equity-financed and 80% debt-financed.
   a. Book building
   b. Rights issue
   c. Market for corporate control
   d. Capital structure

27. _____ is the provision of resources (such as granting a loan) by one party to another party where that second party does not reimburse the first party immediately, thereby generating a debt, and instead arranges either to repay or return those resources (or material(s) of equal value) at a later date. The first party is called a creditor, also known as a lender, while the second party is called a debtor, also known as a borrower.

Movements of financial capital are normally dependent on either _____ or equity transfers.

   a. Comparable
   b. Warrant
   c. Clearing house
   d. Credit

28. A _____ assesses the credit worthiness of an individual, corporation, or even a country. _____s are calculated from financial history and current assets and liabilities. Typically, a _____ tells a lender or investor the probability of the subject being able to pay back a loan.
   a. Credit report monitoring
   b. Credit rating
   c. Debenture
   d. Credit cycle

29. _____ are government bonds issued by the United States Department of the Treasury through the Bureau of the Public Debt. They are the debt financing instruments of the U.S. Federal government, and they are often referred to simply as Treasuries or Treasurys. There are four types of marketable _____: Treasury bills, Treasury notes, Treasury bonds, and Treasury Inflation Protected Securities (TIPS.)
   a. Treasury Inflation Protected Securities
   b. Treasury Inflation-Protected Securities
   c. 4-4-5 Calendar
   d. Treasury securities

30. _____s is a real estate appraisal term referring to properties with characteristics that are similar to a subject property whose value is being sought. This can be accomplished either by a real estate agent who attempts to establish the value of a potential client's home or property through market analysis or, by a licensed or certified appraiser or surveyor using more defined methods, when performing a real estate appraisal.

Chapter 10. Estimating the Cost of Capital

Five factors are usually considered when determining _____s:

- Conditions of Sale -- Did the _____ recently transact under conditions (e.g. -- arms length, distress sale, estate settlement) which are consistent with the standard of value under which the appraisal is being performed?
- Financing Conditions -- Was the _____ transaction influenced by non-market or other favorable (or even unfavorable) financing terms? For example, if the _____ sold with a below-market interest rate provided by the seller, and if the standard of value (e.g. -- market value) assumes no such abnormal financing, then the appraiser may need to adjust the _____ price by an amount equal to the estimated impact of the favorable financing.
- Market Conditions -- This is often referred to as the time adjustment and accounts for changing prices over time.
- Locational Comparability -- Are the _____ and the subject property influenced by the same locational characteristics? For example, even two houses in the same neighborhood may have different views which cause one to be more valuable than the other.
- Physical Comparability -- This includes such factors as size, condition, quality, and age.

A real estate appraisal is like any other statistical sampling process. The _____s are the samples drawn and measured, and the outcome is an estimate of value -- called an 'opinion of value' in the terminology of real estate appraisal.

a. Margin
b. Procter ' Gamble
c. Bucket shop
d. Comparable

31. _____ in business is an accounting concept that refers to ownership of a company (subsidiary) that is less than 50% of outstanding shares. _____ belongs to other investors and is reported on the consolidated balance sheet of the owning company to reflect the claim on assets belonging to other, non-controlling shareholders. Also, _____ is reported on the consolidated income statement as a share of profit belonging to minority shareholders.

a. Minority interest
b. Construction in Progress
c. Credit memo
d. Fixed asset

32. _____ is a fee paid on borrowed assets. It is the price paid for the use of borrowed money , or, money earned by deposited funds . Assets that are sometimes lent with _____ include money, shares, consumer goods through hire purchase, major assets such as aircraft, and even entire factories in finance lease arrangements.

a. Insolvency
b. A Random Walk Down Wall Street
c. AAB
d. Interest

Chapter 11. Calculating and Interpreting Results

1. _____ is a finance term describing a firm's non-Equity cash flows. Theoretically, adding the discounted _____ to the discounted Flows to equity (also known as Equity Cash Flows) will give the firm's Enterprise Value. The Enterprise value is the valuation obtained by calculating the Discounted Cash Flow.
   a. Par value
   b. Foreign exchange hedge
   c. Consignment stock
   d. Debt cash flow

2. In finance, _____ is the process of estimating the potential market value of a financial asset or liability. they can be done on assets (for example, investments in marketable securities such as stocks, options, business enterprises, or intangible assets such as patents and trademarks) or on liabilities (e.g., Bonds issued by a company.) _____s are required in many contexts including investment analysis, capital budgeting, merger and acquisition transactions, financial reporting, taxable events to determine the proper tax liability, and in litigation.
   a. Procter ' Gamble
   b. Margin
   c. Share
   d. Valuation

3. _____ is the balance of the amounts of cash being received and paid by a business during a defined period of time, sometimes tied to a specific project. Measurement of _____ can be used

   - to evaluate the state or performance of a business or project.
   - to determine problems with liquidity. Being profitable does not necessarily mean being liquid. A company can fail because of a shortage of cash, even while profitable.
   - to generate project rate of returns. The time of _____s into and out of projects are used as inputs to financial models such as internal rate of return, and net present value.
   - to examine income or growth of a business when it is believed that accrual accounting concepts do not represent economic realities. Alternately, _____ can be used to 'validate' the net income generated by accrual accounting.

   _____ as a generic term may be used differently depending on context, and certain _____ definitions may be adapted by analysts and users for their own uses. Common terms include operating _____ and free _____.

   _____s can be classified into:

   1. Operational _____s: Cash received or expended as a result of the company's core business activities.
   2. Investment _____s: Cash received or expended through capital expenditure, investments or acquisitions.
   3. Financing _____s: Cash received or expended as a result of financial activities, such as interests and dividends.

   All three together - the net _____ - are necessary to reconcile the beginning cash balance to the ending cash balance. Loan draw downs or equity injections, that is just shifting of capital but no expenditure as such, are not considered in the net _____.

   a. Cash flow
   b. Shareholder value
   c. Corporate finance
   d. Real option

Chapter 11. Calculating and Interpreting Results

4. A '_____' is a 'Charge' that is paid to obtain the right to delay a payment. Essentially, the payer purchases the right to make a given payment in the future instead of in the Present. The '_____', or 'Charge' that must be paid to delay the payment, is simply the difference between what the payment amount would be if it were paid in the present and what the payment amount would be paid if it were paid in the future.
   a. Risk aversion
   b. Discount
   c. Risk modeling
   d. Value at risk

5. In corporate finance, _____ is a cash flow available for distribution among all the security holders of a company. They include equity holders, debt holders, preferred stock holders, convertible security holders, and so on.

   Note that the first three lines above are calculated for you on the standard Statement of Cash Flows.

   a. Forfaiting
   b. Free cash flow
   c. Safety stock
   d. Funding

6. In business and accounting, _____s are everything of value that is owned by a person or company. The balance sheet of a firm records the monetary value of the _____s owned by the firm. The two major _____ classes are tangible _____s and intangible _____s.
   a. Income
   b. Asset
   c. Accounts payable
   d. EBITDA

7. A _____ is a fungible, negotiable instrument representing financial value. They are broadly categorized into debt securities (such as banknotes, bonds and debentures), and equity securities; e.g., common stocks. The company or other entity issuing the _____ is called the issuer.
   a. Securities lending
   b. Book entry
   c. Security
   d. Tracking stock

8. A _____, in business matters, is an entity that is controlled by a bigger and more powerful entity. The controlled entity is called a company, corporation, or limited liability company, and the controlling entity is called its parent (or the parent company.) The reason for this distinction is that a lone company cannot be a _____ of any organization; only an entity representing a legal fiction as a separate entity can be a _____.
   a. 4-4-5 Calendar
   b. Subsidiary
   c. Joint stock company
   d. 529 plan

9. In economics, business, and accounting, a _____ is the value of money that has been used up to produce something, and hence is not available for use anymore. In business, the _____ may be one of acquisition, in which case the amount of money expended to acquire it is counted as _____. In this case, money is the input that is gone in order to acquire the thing.
   a. Sliding scale fees
   b. Fixed costs
   c. Marginal cost
   d. Cost

10. _____ are securities that can be easily converted into cash. Such securities will generally have highly liquid markets allowing the security to be sold at a reasonable price very quickly. This is a usual feature in real estate.
    a. Book entry
    b. Marketable
    c. Tracking stock
    d. Securities lending

Chapter 11. Calculating and Interpreting Results

11. _____ is a term in Corporate Finance used to indicate a condition when promises to creditors of a company are broken or honored with difficulty. Sometimes _____ can lead to bankruptcy. _____ is usually associated with some costs to the company and these are known as Costs of _____.
 a. Commercial paper
 b. Financial distress
 c. Cashflow matching
 d. Capital structure

12. _____ is that which is owed; usually referencing assets owed, but the term can cover other obligations. In the case of assets, _____ is a means of using future purchasing power in the present before a summation has been earned. Some companies and corporations use _____ as a part of their overall corporate finance strategy.
 a. Partial Payment
 b. Debt
 c. Cross-collateralization
 d. Credit cycle

13. Leasing is a process by which a firm can obtain the use of a certain fixed assets for which it must pay a series of contractual, periodic, tax deductible payments. The lessee is the receiver of the services or the assets under the lease contract and the lessor is the owner of the assets. The relationship between the tenant and the landlord is called a _____, and can be for a fixed or an indefinite period of time (called the term of the lease.)
 a. REIT
 b. Real Estate Investment Trust
 c. Tenancy
 d. Real estate investing

14. In financial accounting, _____s are precautions for which the amount or probability of occurrence are not known. Typical examples are _____s for warranty costs and _____ for taxes the term reserve is used instead of term _____; such a use, however, is inconsistent with the terminology suggested by International Accounting Standards Board.
 a. Petty cash
 b. Provision
 c. Momentum Accounting and Triple-Entry Bookkeeping
 d. Money measurement concept

15. An _____ is a lease whose term is short compared to the useful life of the asset or piece of equipment (an airliner, a ship etc.) being leased. An _____ is commonly used to acquire equipment on a relatively short-term basis.
 a. ABN Amro
 b. A Random Walk Down Wall Street
 c. Operating lease
 d. AAB

16. _____ is typically a higher ranking stock than voting shares, and its terms are negotiated between the corporation and the investor.

_____ usually carry no voting rights, but may carry superior priority over common stock in the payment of dividends and upon liquidation. _____ may carry a dividend that is paid out prior to any dividends to common stock holders.

 a. Trade-off theory
 b. Follow-on offering
 c. Second lien loan
 d. Preferred stock

17. _____ are liabilities that may or may not be incurred by an entity depending on the outcome of a future event such as a court case. These liabilities are recorded in a company's accounts and shown in the balance sheet when both probable and reasonably estimable. A footnote to the balance sheet describes the nature and extent of the _____.

Chapter 11. Calculating and Interpreting Results

a. Due-on-sale clause
b. Contingent liabilities
c. 529 plan
d. 4-4-5 Calendar

18. An _____ is a call option on the common stock of a company, issued as a form of non-cash compensation. Restrictions on the option (such as vesting and limited transferability) attempt to align the holder's interest with those of the business' shareholders. If the company's stock rises, holders of options experience a direct financial benefit.
a. Employee stock option
b. Operating ratio
c. Underwriting contract
d. Internal financing

19. An _____ is a contract written by a seller that conveys to the buyer the right -- but not the obligation -- to buy (in the case of a call _____) or to sell (in the case of a put _____) a particular asset, such as a piece of property such as, among others, a futures contract. In return for granting the _____, the seller collects a payment (the premium) from the buyer.

For example, buying a call _____ provides the right to buy a specified quantity of a security at a set strike price at some time on or before expiration, while buying a put _____ provides the right to sell.

a. Annuity
b. AT'T Mobility LLC
c. Amortization
d. Option

20. In finance, a _____ is a type of bond that can be converted into shares of stock in the issuing company, usually at some pre-announced ratio. It is a hybrid security with debt- and equity-like features. Although it typically has a low coupon rate, the holder is compensated with the ability to convert the bond to common stock, usually at a substantial discount to the stock's market value.
a. Bond fund
b. Convertible bond
c. Gilts
d. Corporate bond

21. _____ in business is an accounting concept that refers to ownership of a company (subsidiary) that is less than 50% of outstanding shares. _____ belongs to other investors and is reported on the consolidated balance sheet of the owning company to reflect the claim on assets belonging to other, non-controlling shareholders. Also, _____ is reported on the consolidated income statement as a share of profit belonging to minority shareholders.
a. Credit memo
b. Minority interest
c. Fixed asset
d. Construction in Progress

22. _____ is a fee paid on borrowed assets. It is the price paid for the use of borrowed money , or, money earned by deposited funds . Assets that are sometimes lent with _____ include money, shares, consumer goods through hire purchase, major assets such as aircraft, and even entire factories in finance lease arrangements.
a. AAB
b. Interest
c. Insolvency
d. A Random Walk Down Wall Street

23. In business and finance, a _____ (also referred to as equity _____) of stock means a _____ of ownership in a corporation (company.) In the plural, stocks is often used as a synonym for _____s especially in the United States, but it is less commonly used that way outside of North America.

In the United Kingdom, South Africa, and Australia, stock can also refer to completely different financial instruments such as government bonds or, less commonly, to all kinds of marketable securities.

Chapter 11. Calculating and Interpreting Results

a. Bucket shop
c. Share
b. Margin
d. Procter ' Gamble

24. _____ is the study of how the variation (uncertainty) in the output of a mathematical model can be apportioned, qualitatively or quantitatively, to different sources of variation in the input of a model .

In more general terms uncertainty and sensitivity analyses investigate the robustness of a study when the study includes some form of mathematical modelling. While uncertainty analysis studies the overall uncertainty in the conclusions of the study, _____ tries to identify what source of uncertainty weights more on the study's conclusions.

a. Synthetic CDO
c. Sensitivity analysis
b. Proxy fight
d. Golden parachute

25. Pure _____ is the increase in wealth that an investor has from making an investment, taking into consideration all costs associated with that investment including the opportunity cost of capital.

A key difficulty in measuring profit is in defining costs. Pure economic monetary profits can be zero or negative even in competitive equilibrium when accounted monetized costs exceed monetized price.

a. Operating profit
c. A Random Walk Down Wall Street
b. Economic profit
d. AAB

26. _____ is the difference between price and the costs of bringing to market whatever it is that is accounted as an enterprise (whether by harvest, extraction, manufacture, or purchase) in terms of the component costs of delivered goods and/or services and any operating or other expenses.

A key difficulty in measuring profit is in defining costs. Pure economic monetary profits can be zero or negative even in competitive equilibrium when accounted monetized costs exceed monetized price.

a. AAB
c. A Random Walk Down Wall Street
b. Economic profit
d. Accounting profit

Chapter 12. Using Multiples for Valuation

1. _____s is a real estate appraisal term referring to properties with characteristics that are similar to a subject property whose value is being sought. This can be accomplished either by a real estate agent who attempts to establish the value of a potential client's home or property through market analysis or, by a licensed or certified appraiser or surveyor using more defined methods, when performing a real estate appraisal.

Five factors are usually considered when determining _____s:

- Conditions of Sale -- Did the _____ recently transact under conditions (e.g. -- arms length, distress sale, estate settlement) which are consistent with the standard of value under which the appraisal is being performed?
- Financing Conditions -- Was the _____ transaction influenced by non-market or other favorable (or even unfavorable) financing terms? For example, if the _____ sold with a below-market interest rate provided by the seller, and if the standard of value (e.g. -- market value) assumes no such abnormal financing, then the appraiser may need to adjust the _____ price by an amount equal to the estimated impact of the favorable financing.
- Market Conditions -- This is often referred to as the time adjustment and accounts for changing prices over time.
- Locational Comparability -- Are the _____ and the subject property influenced by the same locational characteristics? For example, even two houses in the same neighborhood may have different views which cause one to be more valuable than the other.
- Physical Comparability -- This includes such factors as size, condition, quality, and age.

A real estate appraisal is like any other statistical sampling process. The _____s are the samples drawn and measured, and the outcome is an estimate of value -- called an 'opinion of value' in the terminology of real estate appraisal.

a. Comparable
c. Bucket shop
b. Procter ' Gamble
d. Margin

2. _____ is a finance term describing a firm's non-Equity cash flows. Theoretically, adding the discounted _____ to the discounted Flows to equity (also known as Equity Cash Flows) will give the firm's Enterprise Value. The Enterprise value is the valuation obtained by calculating the Discounted Cash Flow.
a. Foreign exchange hedge
c. Consignment stock
b. Par value
d. Debt cash flow

3. In finance, _____ is the process of estimating the potential market value of a financial asset or liability. they can be done on assets (for example, investments in marketable securities such as stocks, options, business enterprises, or intangible assets such as patents and trademarks) or on liabilities (e.g., Bonds issued by a company.) _____s are required in many contexts including investment analysis, capital budgeting, merger and acquisition transactions, financial reporting, taxable events to determine the proper tax liability, and in litigation.
a. Valuation
c. Margin
b. Share
d. Procter ' Gamble

Chapter 12. Using Multiples for Valuation

4. A '_____' is a 'Charge' that is paid to obtain the right to delay a payment. Essentially, the payer purchases the right to make a given payment in the future instead of in the Present. The '_____', or 'Charge' that must be paid to delay the payment, is simply the difference between what the payment amount would be if it were paid in the present and what the payment amount would be paid if it were paid in the future.
   a. Risk modeling
   b. Value at risk
   c. Risk aversion
   d. Discount

5. The _____ is a United States government system for classifying industries by a four-digit code. Established in 1937, it is being supplanted by the six-digit North American Industry Classification System, which was released in 1997; however certain government departments and agencies, such as the U.S. Securities and Exchange Commission (SEC), still use the _____ codes.

The following table is from the SEC's site, which allows searching for companies by _____ code in its database of filings.

   a. Standard Industrial Classification
   b. 4-4-5 Calendar
   c. 529 plan
   d. 7-Eleven

6. The _____ of a stock is a measure of the price paid for a share relative to the annual income or profit earned by the firm per share. It is a financial ratio used for valuation: a higher _____ means that investors are paying more for each unit of income, so the stock is more expensive compared to one with lower _____.

The _____ has units of years, which can be interpreted as 'number of years of earnings to pay back purchase price'.

   a. Sustainable growth rate
   b. Return of capital
   c. Quick ratio
   d. P/E ratio

7. An _____ is a lease whose term is short compared to the useful life of the asset or piece of equipment (an airliner, a ship etc.) being leased. An _____ is commonly used to acquire equipment on a relatively short-term basis.
   a. A Random Walk Down Wall Street
   b. ABN Amro
   c. AAB
   d. Operating lease

8. An _____ is a contract written by a seller that conveys to the buyer the right -- but not the obligation -- to buy (in the case of a call _____) or to sell (in the case of a put _____) a particular asset, such as a piece of property such as, among others, a futures contract. In return for granting the _____, the seller collects a payment (the premium) from the buyer.

For example, buying a call _____ provides the right to buy a specified quantity of a security at a set strike price at some time on or before expiration, while buying a put _____ provides the right to sell.

   a. Option
   b. AT'T Mobility LLC
   c. Annuity
   d. Amortization

Chapter 12. Using Multiples for Valuation

9. Leasing is a process by which a firm can obtain the use of a certain fixed assets for which it must pay a series of contractual, periodic, tax deductable payments. The lessee is the receiver of the services or the assets under the lease contract and the lessor is the owner of the assets. The relationship between the tenant and the landlord is called a _____, and can be for a fixed or an indefinite period of time (called the term of the lease.)

   a. Tenancy   b. Real estate investing
   c. Real Estate Investment Trust   d. REIT

10. The _____ (Price/Earnings To Growth ratio) is a valuation metric for determining the relative trade-off between the price of a stock, the earnings generated per share (EPS), and the company's expected growth.

In general, the P/E ratio is higher for a company with a higher growth rate. Thus using just the P/E ratio would make high-growth companies overvalued relative to others.

   a. Return on equity   b. Return on assets
   c. PEG ratio   d. Current ratio

Chapter 13. Performance Measurement

1. _____ is the process whereby an organization establishes the parameters within which programs, investments, and acquisitions are reaching the desired results. Performance Reference Model of the Federal Enterprise Architecture, 2005.

This process of measuring performance ofter requires the use of statistical evidence to determine progress toward specific defined organizational objectives.

There are many types of measurements.

- a. Decentralization
- b. Corporate Transparency
- c. Cash cow
- d. Performance measurement

2. In finance, _____ is the process of estimating the potential market value of a financial asset or liability. they can be done on assets (for example, investments in marketable securities such as stocks, options, business enterprises, or intangible assets such as patents and trademarks) or on liabilities (e.g., Bonds issued by a company.) _____s are required in many contexts including investment analysis, capital budgeting, merger and acquisition transactions, financial reporting, taxable events to determine the proper tax liability, and in litigation.
   - a. Procter ' Gamble
   - b. Margin
   - c. Share
   - d. Valuation

3. A _____ is a private or public market for the trading of company stock and derivatives of company stock at an agreed price; these are securities listed on a stock exchange as well as those only traded privately.

The size of the world _____ is estimated at about $36.6 trillion US at the beginning of October 2008. The world derivatives market has been estimated at about $480 trillion face or nominal value, 12 times the size of the entire world economy.

- a. Adolph Coors
- b. Andrew Tobias
- c. Anton Gelonkin
- d. Stock market

4. _____ is a finance term describing a firm's non-Equity cash flows. Theoretically, adding the discounted _____ to the discounted Flows to equity (also known as Equity Cash Flows) will give the firm's Enterprise Value. The Enterprise value is the valuation obtained by calculating the Discounted Cash Flow.
   - a. Debt cash flow
   - b. Foreign exchange hedge
   - c. Consignment stock
   - d. Par value

5. The _____ is a performance management tool which began as a concept for measuring whether the smaller-scale operational activities of a company are aligned with its larger-scale objectives in terms of vision and strategy.

By focusing not only on financial outcomes but also on the operational, marketing and developmental inputs to these, the _____ helps provide a more comprehensive view of a business, which in turn helps organizations act in their best long-term interests.

Organizations were encouraged to measure--in addition to financial outputs--what influenced such financial outputs.

Chapter 13. Performance Measurement

a. Balanced scorecard
b. Cash cow
c. Decentralization
d. Management by exception

6. In economics, business, and accounting, a _____ is the value of money that has been used up to produce something, and hence is not available for use anymore. In business, the _____ may be one of acquisition, in which case the amount of money expended to acquire it is counted as _____. In this case, money is the input that is gone in order to acquire the thing.
   a. Fixed costs
   b. Marginal cost
   c. Sliding scale fees
   d. Cost

7. In economic models, the _____ time frame assumes no fixed factors of production. Firms can enter or leave the marketplace, and the cost (and availability) of land, labor, raw materials, and capital goods can be assumed to vary. In contrast, in the short-run time frame, certain factors are assumed to be fixed, because there is not sufficient time for them to change.
   a. Short-run
   b. Long-run
   c. 529 plan
   d. 4-4-5 Calendar

8. _____ is the price at which an asset would trade in a competitive Walrasian auction setting. _____ is often used interchangeably with open _____, fair value or fair _____, although these terms have distinct definitions in different standards, and may differ in some circumstances.

International Valuation Standards defines _____ as 'the estimated amount for which a property should exchange on the date of valuation between a willing buyer and a willing seller in an arm'e;s-length transaction after proper marketing wherein the parties had each acted knowledgeably, prudently, and without compulsion.'

_____ is a concept distinct from market price, which is 'e;the price at which one can transact'e;, while _____ is 'e;the true underlying value'e; according to theoretical standards.

   a. T-Model
   b. Wrap account
   c. Debt restructuring
   d. Market value

9. _____ is the difference between the current market value of a firm and the capital contributed by investors. If _____ is positive, the firm has added value. If it is negative, the firm has destroyed value.
   a. Monetary system
   b. Wrap account
   c. Decision process tool
   d. Market value added

10. _____ refers to the additional value of a commodity over the cost of commodities used to produce it from the previous stage of production. An example is the price of gasoline at the pump over the price of the oil in it. In national accounts used in macroeconomics, it refers to the contribution of the factors of production, i.e., land, labor, and capital goods, to raising the value of a product and corresponds to the incomes received by the owners of these factors.
   a. Deregulation
   b. Supply shock
   c. Demand shock
   d. Value added

Chapter 14. Performance Management

1. In corporate finance, _____ is an estimate of true economic profit after making corrective adjustments to GAAP accounting, including deducting the opportunity cost of equity capital. GAAP is estimated to ignore US$300 billion in shareholder opportunity costs. _____ can be measured as Net Operating Profit After Taxes(or NOPAT) less the money cost of capital.
   a. ABN Amro
   b. A Random Walk Down Wall Street
   c. Economic value added
   d. AAB

2. _____ refers to the additional value of a commodity over the cost of commodities used to produce it from the previous stage of production. An example is the price of gasoline at the pump over the price of the oil in it. In national accounts used in macroeconomics, it refers to the contribution of the factors of production, i.e., land, labor, and capital goods, to raising the value of a product and corresponds to the incomes received by the owners of these factors.
   a. Deregulation
   b. Demand shock
   c. Supply shock
   d. Value added

3. _____ is pay or salary, typically monetary payment for services rendered, as in an employment. Usage is considered formal.

   _____ can include:

   - Commission
   - Compensation methods (in online advertising and internet marketing)
   - Compensation
     - Executive compensation
     - Deferred compensation
   - Employee stock option
   - Fringe benefit
   - Salary
   - Wage

   a. Remuneration
   b. 4-4-5 Calendar
   c. 529 plan
   d. 7-Eleven

4. _____ is the process of comparing the cost, time or quality of what one organization does against what another organization does. The result is often a business case for making changes in order to make improvements.

   Also referred to as 'best practice _____' or 'process _____', it is a process used in management and particularly strategic management, in which organizations evaluate various aspects of their processes in relation to best practice, usually within their own sector.

   a. 7-Eleven
   b. 529 plan
   c. 4-4-5 Calendar
   d. Benchmarking

5. _____ is the process whereby an organization establishes the parameters within which programs, investments, and acquisitions are reaching the desired results. Performance Reference Model of the Federal Enterprise Architecture, 2005.

Chapter 14. Performance Management

This process of measuring performance ofter requires the use of statistical evidence to determine progress toward specific defined organizational objectives.

There are many types of measurements.

a. Cash cow
c. Performance measurement

b. Decentralization
d. Corporate Transparency

6. An _____ is a contract written by a seller that conveys to the buyer the right -- but not the obligation -- to buy (in the case of a call _____) or to sell (in the case of a put _____) a particular asset, such as a piece of property such as, among others, a futures contract. In return for granting the _____, the seller collects a payment (the premium) from the buyer.

For example, buying a call _____ provides the right to buy a specified quantity of a security at a set strike price at some time on or before expiration, while buying a put _____ provides the right to sell.

a. Annuity
c. Amortization

b. Option
d. AT'T Mobility LLC

Chapter 15. Creating Value through Mergers and Acquisitions

1. The phrase _____ refers to the aspect of corporate strategy, corporate finance and management dealing with the buying, selling and combining of different companies that can aid, finance, or help a growing company in a given industry grow rapidly without having to create another business entity.

An acquisition, also known as a takeover, is the buying of one company (the 'target') by another. An acquisition may be friendly or hostile.

 a. 4-4-5 Calendar
 b. Mergers and acquisitions
 c. 7-Eleven
 d. 529 plan

2. In finance, _____ is the process of business expansion due to increased output, sales, or both, as opposed to mergers, acquisitions the _____ rate also excludes the impact of foreign exchange. Growth including foreign exchange, but excluding divestitures and acquisitions is often referred to as core growth.
 a. ABN Amro
 b. A Random Walk Down Wall Street
 c. Organic growth
 d. AAB

3. _____ is the price at which an asset would trade in a competitive Walrasian auction setting. _____ is often used interchangeably with open _____, fair value or fair _____, although these terms have distinct definitions in different standards, and may differ in some circumstances.

International Valuation Standards defines _____ as 'the estimated amount for which a property should exchange on the date of valuation between a willing buyer and a willing seller in an arm'e;s-length transaction after proper marketing wherein the parties had each acted knowledgeably, prudently, and without compulsion.'

_____ is a concept distinct from market price, which is 'e;the price at which one can transact'e;, while _____ is 'e;the true underlying value'e; according to theoretical standards.

 a. Wrap account
 b. Market value
 c. T-Model
 d. Debt restructuring

4. In finance, _____ refers to the value of a security which is intrinsic to or contained in the security itself. It is also frequently called fundamental value. It is ordinarily calculated by summing the future income generated by the asset, and discounting it to the present value.
 a. Accretion
 b. Intrinsic value
 c. Amortization
 d. Alpha

5. In economics, collective bargaining, psychology and political science, 'free riders' are those who consume more than their fair share of a resource, or shoulder less than a fair share of the costs of its production. Free riding is usually considered to be an economic 'problem' only when it leads to the non-production or under-production of a public good (and thus to Pareto inefficiency), or when it leads to the excessive use of a common property resource. The _____ is the question of how to prevent free riding from taking place (or at least limit its negative effects) in these situations.
 a. 529 plan
 b. 4-4-5 Calendar
 c. 7-Eleven
 d. Free rider problem

6. _____ is a term used in modern English to indicate overweening pride, superciliousness often resulting in fatal retribution or nemesis. In ancient Greece, _____ referred to actions which, intentionally or not, shamed and humiliated the victim, and frequently the perpetrator as well. It was most evident in the public and private actions of the powerful and rich.

Chapter 15. Creating Value through Mergers and Acquisitions

a. 7-Eleven
c. 4-4-5 Calendar
b. Hubris
d. 529 plan

7. In economics, business, and accounting, a _____ is the value of money that has been used up to produce something, and hence is not available for use anymore. In business, the _____ may be one of acquisition, in which case the amount of money expended to acquire it is counted as _____. In this case, money is the input that is gone in order to acquire the thing.

a. Fixed costs
c. Marginal cost
b. Sliding scale fees
d. Cost

8. _____ is a financial measure that quantifies how well a company generates cash flow relative to the capital it has invested in its business. It is defined as Net operating profit less adjusted taxes divided by Invested Capital and is usually expressed as a percentage. In this calculation, capital invested includes all monetary capital invested: long-term debt, common and preferred shares.

a. Cash conversion cycle
c. Sharpe ratio
b. Debt service coverage ratio
d. Return on invested capital

9. _____ represents the total cash investment that shareholders and debtholders have made in a company. There are two different but completely equivalent methods for calculating _____. The operating approach is calculated as:

_____ = Operating Net Working Capital + Net PP'E + Capitalized Operating Leases + Other Operating Assets + Operating Intangibles - Other Operating Liabilities - Cumulative Adjustment for Amortization of R'D

Equivalently, the financing approach is calculated as:

In symbols:

$$K = D + E - M$$

_____ is used in several important measurements of financial performance, including return on _____, economic value added, and free cash flow.

a. Operating leverage
c. Invested capital
b. Information ratio
d. Inventory turnover

10. In business, _____ is income that a company receives from its normal business activities, usually from the sale of goods and services to customers. Some companies also receive _____ from interest, dividends or royalties paid to them by other companies. _____ may refer to business income in general, or it may refer to the amount, in a monetary unit, received during a period of time, as in 'Last year, Company X had _____ of $32 million.'

In many countries, including the UK, _____ is referred to as turnover.

a. Bottom line
c. Furniture, Fixtures and Equipment
b. Matching principle
d. Revenue

Chapter 15. Creating Value through Mergers and Acquisitions

11. _____ is an accounting term used to reflect the portion of the book value of a business entity not directly attributable to its assets and liabilities; it normally arises only in case of an acquisition. It reflects the ability of the entity to make a higher profit than would be derived from selling the tangible assets. _____ is also known as an intangible asset.

a. Goodwill	b. Cost of goods sold
c. Net profit	d. Consolidation

12. _____ methods are means of managing inventory and financial matters involving the money a company ties up within inventory of produced goods, raw materials, parts, components, or feed stocks.

In LIFO accounting, a historical method of recording the value of inventory, a firm records the last units purchased as the first units sold. LIFO is an acronym for 'last in, first out.' Sometimes the term FILO ('first in, last out') is used synonymously.

a. Payroll	b. General journal
c. Net sales	d. FIFO and LIFO accounting

13. _____ is the process of decreasing an amount over a period of time. The word comes from Middle English amortisen to kill, alienate in mortmain, from Anglo-French amorteser, alteration of amortir, from Vulgar Latin admortire to kill, from Latin ad- + mort-, mors death. Particular instances of the term include:

- _____ (business), the allocation of a lump sum amount to different time periods, particularly for loans and other forms of finance, including related interest or other finance charges.
    - _____ schedule, a table detailing each periodic payment on a loan (typically a mortgage), as generated by an _____ calculator.
    - Negative _____, an _____ schedule where the loan amount actually increases through not paying the full interest
- Amortized analysis, analyzing the execution cost of algorithms over a sequence of operations.
- _____ of capital expenditures of certain assets under accounting rules, particularly intangible assets, in a manner analogous to depreciation.
- _____ (tax law)

_____ is also used in the context of zoning regulations and describes the time in which a property owner has to relocate when the property's use constitutes a preexisting nonconforming use under zoning regulations.

- Depreciation

a. Option	b. Intrinsic value
c. AT'T Inc.	d. Amortization

Chapter 16. Creating Value through Divestitures

1. In finance and economics, _____ or divestiture is the reduction of some kind of asset for either financial goals or ethical objectives. A _____ is the opposite of an investment.

Often the term is used as a means to grow financially in which a company sells off a business unit in order to focus their resources on a market it judges to be more profitable, or promising.

   a. Portfolio investment
   b. Certificate in Investment Performance Measurement
   c. Late trading
   d. Divestment

2. _____, is when a company issues common stock or shares to the public for the first time. They are often issued by smaller, younger companies seeking capital to expand, but can also be done by large privately-owned companies looking to become publicly traded.

In an _____ the issuer may obtain the assistance of an underwriting firm, which helps it determine what type of security to issue (common or preferred), best offering price and time to bring it to market.

   a. Interest
   b. Asian Financial Crisis
   c. Insolvency
   d. Initial public offering

3. A _____ is an entity formed between two or more parties to undertake economic activity together. The parties agree to create a new entity by both contributing equity, and they then share in the revenues, expenses, and control of the enterprise. The venture can be for one specific project only, or a continuing business relationship such as the Sony Ericsson _____.

   a. Fair Debt Collection Practices Act
   b. Pre-emption right
   c. Lien
   d. Joint venture

4. A _____ is a new organization or entity formed by a split from a larger one, such as a television series based on a pre-existing one, or a new company formed from a university research group or business incubator. In literature, especially in milieu-based popular fictional book series like mysteries, westerns, fantasy, or science fiction, the term sub-series is generally used instead of _____, but with essentially the same meaning.

_____s as a descriptive term can also include a dissenting faction of a membership organization, a sect of a cult, or a denomination of a church.

   a. Spin-off
   b. 7-Eleven
   c. 4-4-5 Calendar
   d. 529 plan

5. A _____ is a security issued by a parent company to track the results of one of its subsidiaries or lines of business. The financial results of the subsidiary or line of business are attributed to the _____. Often, the reason for doing so is to separate a high-growth division from a larger parent company.

   a. Securities lending
   b. Tracking stock
   c. Marketable
   d. Book entry

Chapter 17. Capital Structure

1. In finance, _____ refers to the way a corporation finances its assets through some combination of equity, debt, or hybrid securities. A firm's _____ is then the composition or 'structure' of its liabilities. For example, a firm that sells $20 billion in equity and $80 billion in debt is said to be 20% equity-financed and 80% debt-financed.
   a. Book building
   b. Capital structure
   c. Market for corporate control
   d. Rights issue

2. A _____ is a situation that involves losing one quality or aspect of something in return for gaining another quality or aspect. It implies a decision to be made with full comprehension of both the upside and downside of a particular choice.

   In economics the term is expressed as opportunity cost, referring the most preferred alternative given up.

   a. Capital outflow
   b. Break-even point
   c. Total revenue
   d. Trade-off

3. _____ is a legally declared inability or impairment of ability of an individual or organization to pay their creditors. Creditors may file a _____ petition against a debtor ('involuntary _____') in an effort to recoup a portion of what they are owed or initiate a restructuring. In the majority of cases, however, _____ is initiated by the debtor (a 'voluntary _____' that is filed by the bankrupt individual or organization.)
   a. 529 plan
   b. Debt settlement
   c. 4-4-5 Calendar
   d. Bankruptcy

4. In economics, business, and accounting, a _____ is the value of money that has been used up to produce something, and hence is not available for use anymore. In business, the _____ may be one of acquisition, in which case the amount of money expended to acquire it is counted as _____. In this case, money is the input that is gone in order to acquire the thing.
   a. Marginal cost
   b. Cost
   c. Fixed costs
   d. Sliding scale fees

5. _____ is the provision of resources (such as granting a loan) by one party to another party where that second party does not reimburse the first party immediately, thereby generating a debt, and instead arranges either to repay or return those resources (or material(s) of equal value) at a later date. The first party is called a creditor, also known as a lender, while the second party is called a debtor, also known as a borrower.

   Movements of financial capital are normally dependent on either _____ or equity transfers.

   a. Credit
   b. Warrant
   c. Comparable
   d. Clearing house

6. A _____ assesses the credit worthiness of an individual, corporation, or even a country. _____s are calculated from financial history and current assets and liabilities. Typically, a _____ tells a lender or investor the probability of the subject being able to pay back a loan.
   a. Credit rating
   b. Credit report monitoring
   c. Debenture
   d. Credit cycle

7. _____ is an acronym that refers to a company's earnings before the deduction of interest, tax and amortization expenses. It is a financial indicator used widely as a measure of efficiency and profitability.

Chapter 17. Capital Structure

a. AAB
b. ABN Amro
c. A Random Walk Down Wall Street
d. EBITA

8. _____ is the process of decreasing an amount over a period of time. The word comes from Middle English amortisen to kill, alienate in mortmain, from Anglo-French amorteser, alteration of amortir, from Vulgar Latin admortire to kill, from Latin ad- + mort-, mors death. Particular instances of the term include:

- _____ (business), the allocation of a lump sum amount to different time periods, particularly for loans and other forms of finance, including related interest or other finance charges.
    - _____ schedule, a table detailing each periodic payment on a loan (typically a mortgage), as generated by an _____ calculator.
    - Negative _____, an _____ schedule where the loan amount actually increases through not paying the full interest
- Amortized analysis, analyzing the execution cost of algorithms over a sequence of operations.
- _____ of capital expenditures of certain assets under accounting rules, particularly intangible assets, in a manner analogous to depreciation.
- _____ (tax law)

_____ is also used in the context of zoning regulations and describes the time in which a property owner has to relocate when the property's use constitutes a preexisting nonconforming use under zoning regulations.

- Depreciation

a. AT'T Inc.
b. Option
c. Intrinsic value
d. Amortization

9. _____ is a fee paid on borrowed assets. It is the price paid for the use of borrowed money , or, money earned by deposited funds . Assets that are sometimes lent with _____ include money, shares, consumer goods through hire purchase, major assets such as aircraft, and even entire factories in finance lease arrangements.
a. AAB
b. Insolvency
c. A Random Walk Down Wall Street
d. Interest

10. _____ is a finance term describing a firm's non-Equity cash flows. Theoretically, adding the discounted _____ to the discounted Flows to equity (also known as Equity Cash Flows) will give the firm's Enterprise Value. The Enterprise value is the valuation obtained by calculating the Discounted Cash Flow.
a. Debt cash flow
b. Foreign exchange hedge
c. Par value
d. Consignment stock

11. In finance, the _____ approach describes a method of valuing a project, company, or asset using the concepts of the time value of money. All future cash flows are estimated and discounted to give their present values. The discount rate used is generally the appropriate cost of capital and may incorporate judgments of the uncertainty (riskiness) of the future cash flows.
a. Future-oriented
b. Net present value
c. Discounted cash flow
d. Present value of benefits

Chapter 17. Capital Structure

12. In corporate finance, _____ is a cash flow available for distribution among all the security holders of a company. They include equity holders, debt holders, preferred stock holders, convertible security holders, and so on.

Note that the first three lines above are calculated for you on the standard Statement of Cash Flows.

a. Forfaiting
c. Safety stock

b. Funding
d. Free cash flow

13. _____ is the balance of the amounts of cash being received and paid by a business during a defined period of time, sometimes tied to a specific project. Measurement of _____ can be used

- to evaluate the state or performance of a business or project.
- to determine problems with liquidity. Being profitable does not necessarily mean being liquid. A company can fail because of a shortage of cash, even while profitable.
- to generate project rate of returns. The time of _____s into and out of projects are used as inputs to financial models such as internal rate of return, and net present value.
- to examine income or growth of a business when it is believed that accrual accounting concepts do not represent economic realities. Alternately, _____ can be used to 'validate' the net income generated by accrual accounting.

_____ as a generic term may be used differently depending on context, and certain _____ definitions may be adapted by analysts and users for their own uses. Common terms include operating _____ and free _____.

_____s can be classified into:

1. Operational _____s: Cash received or expended as a result of the company's core business activities.
2. Investment _____s: Cash received or expended through capital expenditure, investments or acquisitions.
3. Financing _____s: Cash received or expended as a result of financial activities, such as interests and dividends.

All three together - the net _____ - are necessary to reconcile the beginning cash balance to the ending cash balance. Loan draw downs or equity injections, that is just shifting of capital but no expenditure as such, are not considered in the net _____.

a. Real option
c. Shareholder value

b. Cash flow
d. Corporate finance

14. In finance, a _____ is a debt security, in which the authorized issuer owes the holders a debt and, depending on the terms of the _____, is obliged to pay interest (the coupon) and/or to repay the principal at a later date, termed maturity.

Thus a _____ is a loan: the issuer is the borrower, the _____ holder is the lender, and the coupon is the interest. _____s provide the borrower with external funds to finance long-term investments, or, in the case of government _____s, to finance current expenditure.

Chapter 17. Capital Structure

a. Catastrophe bonds
b. Convertible bond
c. Puttable bond
d. Bond

15. In finance, _____ (or gearing) is borrowing money to supplement existing funds for investment in such a way that the potential positive or negative outcome is magnified and/or enhanced. It generally refers to using borrowed funds, or debt, so as to attempt to increase the returns to equity. Deleveraging is the action of reducing borrowings.
   a. Limited partnership
   b. Financial endowment
   c. Pension fund
   d. Leverage

16. In finance, _____ is the ability of an entity to pay its debts with available cash. _____ can also be described as the ability of a corporation to meet its long-term fixed expenses and to accomplish long-term expansion and growth. The better a company's _____, the better it is financially.
   a. Solvency
   b. Political risk
   c. Capital asset
   d. Mid price

17. In finance, _____ occurs when a debtor has not met its legal obligations according to the debt contract, e.g. it has not made a scheduled payment, or has violated a loan covenant (condition) of the debt contract. _____ may occur if the debtor is either unwilling or unable to pay their debt. This can occur with all debt obligations including bonds, mortgages, loans, and promissory notes.
   a. Debt validation
   b. Vendor finance
   c. Credit crunch
   d. Default

18. _____ is a parameter used in the calculation of economic capital or regulatory capital under Basel II for a banking institution. This is an attribute of a bank's client.

The _____ is the likelihood that a loan will not be repaid and will fall into default.

   a. Variable rate mortgage
   b. Deposit insurance
   c. Credit bureau
   d. Probability of default

19. _____ is that which is owed; usually referencing assets owed, but the term can cover other obligations. In the case of assets, _____ is a means of using future purchasing power in the present before a summation has been earned. Some companies and corporations use _____ as a part of their overall corporate finance strategy.
   a. Debt
   b. Credit cycle
   c. Partial Payment
   d. Cross-collateralization

20. _____ or financing is to provide capital (funds), which means money for a project, a person, a business or any other private or public institutions.

Those funds can be allocated for either short term or long term purposes. The health fund is a new way of _____ private healthcare centers.

   a. Proxy fight
   b. Synthetic CDO
   c. Product life cycle
   d. Funding

Chapter 17. Capital Structure

21. In economics and related disciplines, a _____ is a cost incurred in making an economic exchange. For example, most people, when buying or selling a stock, must pay a commission to their broker; that commission is a _____ of doing the stock deal. Or consider buying a banana from a store; to purchase the banana, your costs will be not only the price of the banana itself, but also the energy and effort it requires to find out which of the various banana products you prefer, where to get them and at what price, the cost of traveling from your house to the store and back, the time waiting in line, and the effort of the paying itself; the costs above and beyond the cost of the banana are the _____s.

   a. Marginal cost
   b. Fixed costs
   c. Transaction cost
   d. Variable costs

22. In finance, the _____ is the minimum rate of return a firm must offer shareholders to compensate for waiting for their returns, and for bearing some risk.

The _____ capital for a particular company is the rate of return on investment that is required by the company's ordinary shareholders. The return consists both of dividend and capital gains, e.g. increases in the share price.

   a. Cost of equity
   b. Residual value
   c. Net pay
   d. Round-tripping

23. A _____ is a payment made by a corporation to its shareholder members. When a corporation earns a profit or surplus, that money can be put to two uses: it can either be re-invested in the business (called retained earnings), or it can be paid to the shareholders as a _____. Many corporations retain a portion of their earnings and pay the remainder as a _____.

   a. Special dividend
   b. Dividend puzzle
   c. Dividend yield
   d. Dividend

24. The _____ is a United States government system for classifying industries by a four-digit code. Established in 1937, it is being supplanted by the six-digit North American Industry Classification System, which was released in 1997; however certain government departments and agencies, such as the U.S. Securities and Exchange Commission (SEC), still use the _____ codes.

The following table is from the SEC's site, which allows searching for companies by _____ code in its database of filings.

   a. 529 plan
   b. 4-4-5 Calendar
   c. Standard Industrial Classification
   d. 7-Eleven

25. In business and finance, a _____ (also referred to as equity _____) of stock means a _____ of ownership in a corporation (company.) In the plural, stocks is often used as a synonym for _____s especially in the United States, but it is less commonly used that way outside of North America.

In the United Kingdom, South Africa, and Australia, stock can also refer to completely different financial instruments such as government bonds or, less commonly, to all kinds of marketable securities.

Chapter 17. Capital Structure

a. Margin
c. Procter ' Gamble
b. Bucket shop
d. Share

26. In some countries, including the United States and the United Kingdom, corporations can buy back their own stock in a share repurchase, also known as a _____ or share buyback. There has been a meteoric rise in the use of share repurchases in the U.S. in the past twenty years, from $5b in 1980 to $349b in 2005. A share repurchase distributes cash to existing shareholders in exchange for a fraction of the firm's outstanding equity.

a. Trading curb
c. Stock repurchase
b. Common stock
d. Stockholder

27. In finance, _____ is the process of estimating the potential market value of a financial asset or liability. they can be done on assets (for example, investments in marketable securities such as stocks, options, business enterprises, or intangible assets such as patents and trademarks) or on liabilities (e.g., Bonds issued by a company.) _____s are required in many contexts including investment analysis, capital budgeting, merger and acquisition transactions, financial reporting, taxable events to determine the proper tax liability, and in litigation.

a. Valuation
c. Procter ' Gamble
b. Margin
d. Share

28. The institution most often referenced by the word '_____' is a public or publicly traded _____, the shares of which are traded on a public stock exchange (e.g., the New York Stock Exchange or Nasdaq in the United States) where shares of stock of _____s are bought and sold by and to the general public. Most of the largest businesses in the world are publicly traded _____s. However, the majority of _____s are said to be closely held, privately held or close _____s, meaning that no ready market exists for the trading of shares.

a. Depository Trust Company
c. Federal Home Loan Mortgage Corporation
b. Protect
d. Corporation

29. A _____ is a financial contract whose value is derived from the value of something else (known as the underlying.) The underlying on which a _____ is based can be an asset, weather conditions bonds or other forms of credit.

a. 529 plan
c. Derivative
b. 7-Eleven
d. 4-4-5 Calendar

30. Procter is a surname, and may also refer to:

- Bryan Waller Procter (pseud. Barry Cornwall), English poet
- Goodwin Procter, American law firm
- _____, consumer products multinational

a. Clearing house
c. Valuation
b. Bucket shop
d. Procter ' Gamble

31. In finance, a _____ is a type of bond that can be converted into shares of stock in the issuing company, usually at some pre-announced ratio. It is a hybrid security with debt- and equity-like features. Although it typically has a low coupon rate, the holder is compensated with the ability to convert the bond to common stock, usually at a substantial discount to the stock's market value.

a. Gilts
b. Convertible bond
c. Bond fund
d. Corporate bond

32. _____ is typically a higher ranking stock than voting shares, and its terms are negotiated between the corporation and the investor.

_____ usually carry no voting rights, but may carry superior priority over common stock in the payment of dividends and upon liquidation. _____ may carry a dividend that is paid out prior to any dividends to common stock holders.

a. Trade-off theory
b. Second lien loan
c. Follow-on offering
d. Preferred stock

Chapter 18. Investor Communications

1. _____ is the price at which an asset would trade in a competitive Walrasian auction setting. _____ is often used interchangeably with open _____, fair value or fair _____, although these terms have distinct definitions in different standards, and may differ in some circumstances.

International Valuation Standards defines _____ as 'the estimated amount for which a property should exchange on the date of valuation between a willing buyer and a willing seller in an arm'e;s-length transaction after proper marketing wherein the parties had each acted knowledgeably, prudently, and without compulsion.'

_____ is a concept distinct from market price, which is 'e;the price at which one can transact'e;, while _____ is 'e;the true underlying value'e; according to theoretical standards.

- a. Debt restructuring
- b. T-Model
- c. Wrap account
- d. Market value

2. In finance, _____ refers to the value of a security which is intrinsic to or contained in the security itself. It is also frequently called fundamental value. It is ordinarily calculated by summing the future income generated by the asset, and discounting it to the present value.
- a. Amortization
- b. Alpha
- c. Accretion
- d. Intrinsic value

3. In finance and economics, _____ or divestiture is the reduction of some kind of asset for either financial goals or ethical objectives. A _____ is the opposite of an investment.

Often the term is used as a means to grow financially in which a company sells off a business unit in order to focus their resources on a market it judges to be more profitable, or promising.

- a. Portfolio investment
- b. Late trading
- c. Certificate in Investment Performance Measurement
- d. Divestment

4. The phrase _____ refers to the aspect of corporate strategy, corporate finance and management dealing with the buying, selling and combining of different companies that can aid, finance, or help a growing company in a given industry grow rapidly without having to create another business entity.

An acquisition, also known as a takeover, is the buying of one company (the 'target') by another. An acquisition may be friendly or hostile.

- a. 7-Eleven
- b. Mergers and acquisitions
- c. 4-4-5 Calendar
- d. 529 plan

5. In finance, _____ is the process of estimating the potential market value of a financial asset or liability. they can be done on assets (for example, investments in marketable securities such as stocks, options, business enterprises, or intangible assets such as patents and trademarks) or on liabilities (e.g., Bonds issued by a company.) _____s are required in many contexts including investment analysis, capital budgeting, merger and acquisition transactions, financial reporting, taxable events to determine the proper tax liability, and in litigation.
- a. Procter ' Gamble
- b. Margin
- c. Share
- d. Valuation

Chapter 18. Investor Communications

6. _____ consists of the sale of goods or merchandise from a fixed location, such as a department store, boutique or kiosk in small or individual lots for direct consumption by the purchaser. _____ may include subordinated services, such as delivery. Purchasers may be individuals or businesses.
    a. Retailing
    b. 7-Eleven
    c. 529 plan
    d. 4-4-5 Calendar

7. In finance, a _____ is a position established in one market in an attempt to offset exposure to the price risk of an equal but opposite obligation or position in another market -- usually, but not always, in the context of one's commercial activity. Hedging is a strategy designed to minimize exposure to such business risks as a sharp contraction in demand for one's inventory, while still allowing the business to profit from producing and maintaining that inventory. A typical hedger might be a farmer with 2000 acres of unharvested wheat in the ground, who would rather tend his crop without the distraction of uncertain prices.
    a. 529 plan
    b. 4-4-5 Calendar
    c. 7-Eleven
    d. Hedge

8. A _____ is a private investment fund open to a limited range of investors that is permitted by regulators to undertake a wider range of activities than other investment funds and also pays a performance fee to its investment manager. Each fund will have its own strategy which determines the type of investments and the methods of investment it undertakes. _____s as a class invest in a broad range of investments extending over shares, debt, commodities and beyond.
    a. 4-4-5 Calendar
    b. 7-Eleven
    c. 529 plan
    d. Hedge fund

9. _____ are organizations which pool large sums of money and invest those sums in companies. They include banks, insurance companies, retirement or pension funds, hedge funds and mutual funds. Their role in the economy is to act as highly specialized investors on behalf of others.
    a. ABN Amro
    b. Institutional investors
    c. A Random Walk Down Wall Street
    d. AAB

10. _____, refers to consumption opportunity gained by an entity within a specified time frame, which is generally expressed in monetary terms. However, for households and individuals, '_____ is the sum of all the wages, salaries, profits, interests payments, rents and other forms of earnings received... in a given period of time.' For firms, _____ generally refers to net-profit: what remains of revenue after expenses have been subtracted.
    a. Accrual
    b. Annual report
    c. OIBDA
    d. Income

11. _____ is a financial strategy in which a fund manager makes as few portfolio decisions as possible, in order to minimize transaction costs, including the incidence of capital gains tax. One popular method is to mimic the performance of an externally specified index--called 'index funds'. The ethos of an index fund is aptly summed up in the injunction to an index fund manager: 'Don't just do something, sit there!'

_____ is most common on the equity market, where index funds track a stock market index, but it is becoming more common in other investment types, including bonds, commodities and hedge funds.

a. Trust company
b. Savings and loan association
c. Net asset value
d. Passive management

12. _____ refers to different style characteristics of equities, bonds or financial derivatives within a given investment philosophy.

Theory would favor a combination of big capitalization, passive and value. Of course one could almost get that when investing in an important Index like S'P 500, Euro-Stoxx or the like.

a. ABN Amro
b. AAB
c. A Random Walk Down Wall Street
d. Investment style

Chapter 19. Valuing Multibusiness Companies

1. Procter is a surname, and may also refer to:

   - Bryan Waller Procter (pseud. Barry Cornwall), English poet
   - Goodwin Procter, American law firm
   - _____, consumer products multinational

   a. Bucket shop
   b. Valuation
   c. Clearing house
   d. Procter ' Gamble

2. In financial accounting, a _____ or statement of financial position is a summary of a person's or organization's balances. Assets, liabilities and ownership equity are listed as of a specific date, such as the end of its financial year. A _____ is often described as a snapshot of a company's financial condition.

   a. Statement on Auditing Standards No. 70: Service Organizations
   b. Statement of retained earnings
   c. Financial statements
   d. Balance sheet

3. _____ are formal records of a business' financial activities.

   _____ provide an overview of a business' financial condition in both short and long term. There are four basic _____:

   1. **Balance sheet**: also referred to as statement of financial position or condition, reports on a company's assets, liabilities, and net equity as of a given point in time.
   2. **Income statement**: also referred to as Profit and Loss statement (or a 'P'L'), reports on a company's income, expenses, and profits over a period of time.
   3. **Statement of retained earnings**: explains the changes in a company's retained earnings over the reporting period.
   4. **Statement of cash flows**: reports on a company's cash flow activities, particularly its operating, investing and financing activities.

   a. Notes to the Financial Statements
   b. Statement of retained earnings
   c. Financial statements
   d. Statement on Auditing Standards No. 70: Service Organizations

4. _____, refers to consumption opportunity gained by an entity within a specified time frame, which is generally expressed in monetary terms. However, for households and individuals, '_____ is the sum of all the wages, salaries, profits, interests payments, rents and other forms of earnings received... in a given period of time.' For firms, _____ generally refers to net-profit: what remains of revenue after expenses have been subtracted.

   a. OIBDA
   b. Annual report
   c. Income
   d. Accrual

5. An _____ is a financial statement for companies that indicates how Revenue is transformed into net income The purpose of the _____ is to show managers and investors whether the company made or lost money during the period being reported.

   The important thing to remember about an _____ is that it represents a period of time.

Chapter 19. Valuing Multibusiness Companies

a. AAB
b. Income statement
c. A Random Walk Down Wall Street
d. ABN Amro

6. A _____, in business matters, is an entity that is controlled by a bigger and more powerful entity. The controlled entity is called a company, corporation, or limited liability company, and the controlling entity is called its parent (or the parent company.) The reason for this distinction is that a lone company cannot be a _____ of any organization; only an entity representing a legal fiction as a separate entity can be a _____.
   a. 529 plan
   b. Joint stock company
   c. 4-4-5 Calendar
   d. Subsidiary

7. In finance, _____ is the process of estimating the potential market value of a financial asset or liability. they can be done on assets (for example, investments in marketable securities such as stocks, options, business enterprises, or intangible assets such as patents and trademarks) or on liabilities (e.g., Bonds issued by a company.) _____s are required in many contexts including investment analysis, capital budgeting, merger and acquisition transactions, financial reporting, taxable events to determine the proper tax liability, and in litigation.
   a. Procter ' Gamble
   b. Margin
   c. Share
   d. Valuation

8. _____ represents the total cash investment that shareholders and debtholders have made in a company. There are two different but completely equivalent methods for calculating _____. The operating approach is calculated as:

_____ = Operating Net Working Capital + Net PP'E + Capitalized Operating Leases + Other Operating Assets + Operating Intangibles - Other Operating Liabilities - Cumulative Adjustment for Amortization of R'D

Equivalently, the financing approach is calculated as:

In symbols:

$$K = D + E - M$$

_____ is used in several important measurements of financial performance, including return on _____, economic value added, and free cash flow.

   a. Invested capital
   b. Operating leverage
   c. Inventory turnover
   d. Information ratio

9. In economics, business, and accounting, a _____ is the value of money that has been used up to produce something, and hence is not available for use anymore. In business, the _____ may be one of acquisition, in which case the amount of money expended to acquire it is counted as _____. In this case, money is the input that is gone in order to acquire the thing.
   a. Fixed costs
   b. Marginal cost
   c. Sliding scale fees
   d. Cost

10. The _____ is an expected return that the provider of capital plans to earn on their investment.

Chapter 19. Valuing Multibusiness Companies

Capital (money) used for funding a business should earn returns for the capital providers who risk their capital. For an investment to be worthwhile, the expected return on capital must be greater than the _____.

a. 4-4-5 Calendar
c. Capital intensity

b. Weighted average cost of capital
d. Cost of capital

Chapter 20. Valuing Flexibility

1. A _____ is a decision support tool that uses a tree-like graph or model of decisions and their possible consequences, including chance event outcomes, resource costs, and utility. _____s are commonly used in operations research, specifically in decision analysis, to help identify a strategy most likely to reach a goal. Another use of _____s is as a descriptive means for calculating conditional probabilities.

   a. 529 plan
   b. 7-Eleven
   c. Decision tree
   d. 4-4-5 Calendar

2. In finance, _____ is the process of estimating the potential market value of a financial asset or liability. they can be done on assets (for example, investments in marketable securities such as stocks, options, business enterprises, or intangible assets such as patents and trademarks) or on liabilities (e.g., Bonds issued by a company.) _____s are required in many contexts including investment analysis, capital budgeting, merger and acquisition transactions, financial reporting, taxable events to determine the proper tax liability, and in litigation.

   a. Share
   b. Procter ' Gamble
   c. Margin
   d. Valuation

3. _____ or net present worth (NPW) is defined as the total present value (PV) of a time series of cash flows. It is a standard method for using the time value of money to appraise long-term projects. Used for capital budgeting, and widely throughout economics, it measures the excess or shortfall of cash flows, in present value terms, once financing charges are met.

   a. Negative gearing
   b. Present value of costs
   c. Tax shield
   d. Net present value

4. _____ is the value on a given date of a future payment or series of future payments, discounted to reflect the time value of money and other factors such as investment risk. _____ calculations are widely used in business and economics to provide a means to compare cash flows at different times on a meaningful 'like to like' basis.

   The most commonly applied model of the time value of money is compound interest.

   a. Negative gearing
   b. Present value of benefits
   c. Net present value
   d. Present value

5. The _____ is the interest rate that it is assumed can be obtained by investing in financial instruments with no default risk. However, the financial instrument can carry other types of risk, e.g. market risk (the risk of changes in market interest rates), liquidity risk (the risk of being unable to sell the instrument for cash at short notice without significant costs) etc.

   Though a truly risk-free asset exists only in theory, in practice most professionals and academics use short-dated government bonds of the currency in question.

   a. London Interbank Bid Rate
   b. Risk-free interest rate
   c. London Interbank Offered Rate
   d. Cash accumulation equation

6. In economics, business, and accounting, a _____ is the value of money that has been used up to produce something, and hence is not available for use anymore. In business, the _____ may be one of acquisition, in which case the amount of money expended to acquire it is counted as _____. In this case, money is the input that is gone in order to acquire the thing.

Chapter 20. Valuing Flexibility

a. Marginal cost
b. Cost
c. Sliding scale fees
d. Fixed costs

7. _____ is a fee paid on borrowed assets. It is the price paid for the use of borrowed money, or, money earned by deposited funds. Assets that are sometimes lent with _____ include money, shares, consumer goods through hire purchase, major assets such as aircraft, and even entire factories in finance lease arrangements.
  a. A Random Walk Down Wall Street
  b. Insolvency
  c. Interest
  d. AAB

8. An _____ is the price a borrower pays for the use of money they do not own, and the return a lender receives for deferring the use of funds, by lending it to the borrower. _____s are normally expressed as a percentage rate over the period of one year.

_____s targets are also a vital tool of monetary policy and are used to control variables like investment, inflation, and unemployment.

  a. AAB
  b. A Random Walk Down Wall Street
  c. ABN Amro
  d. Interest rate

9. In corporate finance, _____ analysis applies put option and call option valuation techniques to capital budgeting decisions. A _____ itself, is the right--but not the obligation--to undertake some business decision; typically the option to make, or abandon, a capital investment. For example, the opportunity to invest in the expansion of a firm's factory, or alternatively to sell the factory, is a _____.
  a. Book building
  b. Cash flow
  c. Real option
  d. Capital budgeting

10. _____ is the balance of the amounts of cash being received and paid by a business during a defined period of time, sometimes tied to a specific project. Measurement of _____ can be used

- to evaluate the state or performance of a business or project.
- to determine problems with liquidity. Being profitable does not necessarily mean being liquid. A company can fail because of a shortage of cash, even while profitable.
- to generate project rate of returns. The time of _____s into and out of projects are used as inputs to financial models such as internal rate of return, and net present value.
- to examine income or growth of a business when it is believed that accrual accounting concepts do not represent economic realities. Alternately, _____ can be used to 'validate' the net income generated by accrual accounting.

_____ as a generic term may be used differently depending on context, and certain _____ definitions may be adapted by analysts and users for their own uses. Common terms include operating _____ and free _____.

_____s can be classified into:

1. Operational _____s: Cash received or expended as a result of the company's core business activities.
2. Investment _____s: Cash received or expended through capital expenditure, investments or acquisitions.
3. Financing _____s: Cash received or expended as a result of financial activities, such as interests and dividends.

All three together - the net _____ - are necessary to reconcile the beginning cash balance to the ending cash balance. Loan draw downs or equity injections, that is just shifting of capital but no expenditure as such, are not considered in the net _____.

a. Corporate finance
b. Real option
c. Shareholder value
d. Cash flow

11. In finance, the _____ approach describes a method of valuing a project, company, or asset using the concepts of the time value of money. All future cash flows are estimated and discounted to give their present values. The discount rate used is generally the appropriate cost of capital and may incorporate judgments of the uncertainty (riskiness) of the future cash flows.

a. Net present value
b. Discounted cash flow
c. Future-oriented
d. Present value of benefits

12. An _____ is a contract written by a seller that conveys to the buyer the right -- but not the obligation -- to buy (in the case of a call _____) or to sell (in the case of a put _____) a particular asset, such as a piece of property such as, among others, a futures contract. In return for granting the _____, the seller collects a payment (the premium) from the buyer.

For example, buying a call _____ provides the right to buy a specified quantity of a security at a set strike price at some time on or before expiration, while buying a put _____ provides the right to sell.

a. Annuity
b. Amortization
c. AT'T Mobility LLC
d. Option

Chapter 21. Cross-Border Valuation

1. _____ is the standard framework of guidelines for financial accounting used in the United States of America. It includes the standards, conventions, and rules accountants follow in recording and summarizing transactions, and in the preparation of financial statements. _____ are now issued by the Financial Accounting Standards Board (FASB).
   a. Net income
   b. Generally Accepted Accounting Principles
   c. Depreciation
   d. Revenue

2. The U.S. _____ is an independent agency of the United States government which holds primary responsibility for enforcing the federal securities laws and regulating the securities industry, the nation's stock and options exchanges, and other electronic securities markets. The SEC was created by section 4 of the SEC of 1934 (now codified as 15 U.S.C. § 78d and commonly referred to as the 1934 Act.)
   a. 4-4-5 Calendar
   b. 7-Eleven
   c. Securities and Exchange Commission
   d. 529 plan

3. In finance, _____ is the process of estimating the potential market value of a financial asset or liability. they can be done on assets (for example, investments in marketable securities such as stocks, options, business enterprises, or intangible assets such as patents and trademarks) or on liabilities (e.g., Bonds issued by a company.) _____s are required in many contexts including investment analysis, capital budgeting, merger and acquisition transactions, financial reporting, taxable events to determine the proper tax liability, and in litigation.
   a. Procter ' Gamble
   b. Share
   c. Margin
   d. Valuation

4. _____ or amalgamation is the act of merging many things into one. In business, it often refers to the mergers or acquisitions of many smaller companies into much larger ones. The financial accounting term of _____ refers to the aggregated financial statements of a group company as consolidated account.
   a. Write-off
   b. Retained earnings
   c. Cost of goods sold
   d. Consolidation

5. In financial accounting, a _____ or statement of financial position is a summary of a person's or organization's balances. Assets, liabilities and ownership equity are listed as of a specific date, such as the end of its financial year. A _____ is often described as a snapshot of a company's financial condition.
   a. Statement of retained earnings
   b. Statement on Auditing Standards No. 70: Service Organizations
   c. Financial statements
   d. Balance sheet

6. A _____ is a financial contract whose value is derived from the value of something else (known as the underlying.) The underlying on which a _____ is based can be an asset, weather conditions bonds or other forms of credit.
   a. Derivative
   b. 4-4-5 Calendar
   c. 7-Eleven
   d. 529 plan

7. In finance, a _____ is a position established in one market in an attempt to offset exposure to the price risk of an equal but opposite obligation or position in another market -- usually, but not always, in the context of one's commercial activity. Hedging is a strategy designed to minimize exposure to such business risks as a sharp contraction in demand for one's inventory, while still allowing the business to profit from producing and maintaining that inventory. A typical hedger might be a farmer with 2000 acres of unharvested wheat in the ground, who would rather tend his crop without the distraction of uncertain prices.

a. 7-Eleven
b. 529 plan
c. 4-4-5 Calendar
d. Hedge

8. _____, refers to consumption opportunity gained by an entity within a specified time frame, which is generally expressed in monetary terms. However, for households and individuals, '_____ is the sum of all the wages, salaries, profits, interests payments, rents and other forms of earnings received... in a given period of time.' For firms, _____ generally refers to net-profit: what remains of revenue after expenses have been subtracted.
a. Accrual
b. Annual report
c. OIBDA
d. Income

9. An _____ is a financial statement for companies that indicates how Revenue is transformed into net income The purpose of the _____ is to show managers and investors whether the company made or lost money during the period being reported.

The important thing to remember about an _____ is that it represents a period of time.

a. Income statement
b. A Random Walk Down Wall Street
c. ABN Amro
d. AAB

10. _____ are defined as identifiable non-monetary assets that cannot be seen, touched or physically measured, which are created through time and/or effort and that are identifiable as a separate asset. There are two primary forms of intangibles - legal intangibles (such as trade secrets (e.g., customer lists), copyrights, patents, trademarks, and goodwill) and competitive intangibles (such as knowledge activities (know-how, knowledge), collaboration activities, leverage activities, and structural activities.) Legal intangibles generate legal property rights defensible in a court of law.
a. A Random Walk Down Wall Street
b. Intangible assets
c. AAB
d. ABN Amro

11. _____ is a list for goods and materials held available in stock by a business. It is also used for a list of the contents of a household and for a list for testamentary purposes of the possessions of someone who has died. In accounting _____ is considered an asset.
a. ABN Amro
b. AAB
c. A Random Walk Down Wall Street
d. Inventory

12. _____ methods are means of managing inventory and financial matters involving the money a company ties up within inventory of produced goods, raw materials, parts, components, or feed stocks.

In LIFO accounting, a historical method of recording the value of inventory, a firm records the last units purchased as the first units sold. LIFO is an acronym for 'last in, first out.' Sometimes the term FILO ('first in, last out') is used synonymously.

a. General journal
b. Payroll
c. Net sales
d. FIFO and LIFO accounting

Chapter 21. Cross-Border Valuation

13. Leasing is a process by which a firm can obtain the use of a certain fixed assets for which it must pay a series of contractual, periodic, tax deductable payments. The lessee is the receiver of the services or the assets under the lease contract and the lessor is the owner of the assets. The relationship between the tenant and the landlord is called a _____, and can be for a fixed or an indefinite period of time (called the term of the lease.)
   - a. Tenancy
   - b. Real estate investing
   - c. REIT
   - d. Real Estate Investment Trust

14. _____ is a financial measure that quantifies how well a company generates cash flow relative to the capital it has invested in its business. It is defined as Net operating profit less adjusted taxes divided by Invested Capital and is usually expressed as a percentage. In this calculation, capital invested includes all monetary capital invested: long-term debt, common and preferred shares.
   - a. Cash conversion cycle
   - b. Sharpe ratio
   - c. Debt service coverage ratio
   - d. Return on invested capital

15. In business and accounting, _____s are everything of value that is owned by a person or company. The balance sheet of a firm records the monetary value of the _____s owned by the firm. The two major _____ classes are tangible _____s and intangible _____s.
   - a. Accounts payable
   - b. EBITDA
   - c. Income
   - d. Asset

16. An _____ is a call option on the common stock of a company, issued as a form of non-cash compensation. Restrictions on the option (such as vesting and limited transferability) attempt to align the holder's interest with those of the business' shareholders. If the company's stock rises, holders of options experience a direct financial benefit.
   - a. Operating ratio
   - b. Internal financing
   - c. Underwriting contract
   - d. Employee stock option

17. _____ plant, and equipment, is a term used in accountancy for assets and property which cannot easily be converted into cash. This can be compared with current assets such as cash or bank accounts, which are described as liquid assets. In most cases, only tangible assets are referred to as fixed.
   - a. Percentage of Completion
   - b. Remittance advice
   - c. Petty cash
   - d. Fixed asset

18. _____ is an accounting term used to reflect the portion of the book value of a business entity not directly attributable to its assets and liabilities; it normally arises only in case of an acquisition. It reflects the ability of the entity to make a higher profit than would be derived from selling the tangible assets. _____ is also known as an intangible asset.
   - a. Goodwill
   - b. Consolidation
   - c. Cost of goods sold
   - d. Net profit

19. _____ represents the total cash investment that shareholders and debtholders have made in a company. There are two different but completely equivalent methods for calculating _____. The operating approach is calculated as:

_____ = Operating Net Working Capital + Net PP'E + Capitalized Operating Leases + Other Operating Assets + Operating Intangibles - Other Operating Liabilities - Cumulative Adjustment for Amortization of R'D

Equivalently, the financing approach is calculated as:

In symbols:

$$K = D + E - M$$

_____ is used in several important measurements of financial performance, including return on _____, economic value added, and free cash flow.

a. Operating leverage
c. Invested capital
b. Information ratio
d. Inventory turnover

20. An _____ is a contract written by a seller that conveys to the buyer the right -- but not the obligation -- to buy (in the case of a call _____) or to sell (in the case of a put _____) a particular asset, such as a piece of property such as, among others, a futures contract. In return for granting the _____, the seller collects a payment (the premium) from the buyer.

For example, buying a call _____ provides the right to buy a specified quantity of a security at a set strike price at some time on or before expiration, while buying a put _____ provides the right to sell.

a. Annuity
c. Option
b. Amortization
d. AT'T Mobility LLC

21. In financial accounting, _____s are precautions for which the amount or probability of occurrence are not known. Typical examples are _____s for warranty costs and _____ for taxes the term reserve is used instead of term _____; such a use, however, is inconsistent with the terminology suggested by International Accounting Standards Board.

a. Petty cash
c. Provision
b. Momentum Accounting and Triple-Entry Bookkeeping
d. Money measurement concept

22. In business, _____ is income that a company receives from its normal business activities, usually from the sale of goods and services to customers. Some companies also receive _____ from interest, dividends or royalties paid to them by other companies. _____ may refer to business income in general, or it may refer to the amount, in a monetary unit, received during a period of time, as in 'Last year, Company X had _____ of $32 million.'

In many countries, including the UK, _____ is referred to as turnover.

a. Matching principle
c. Furniture, Fixtures and Equipment
b. Bottom line
d. Revenue

23. The _____ principle is a cornerstone of accrual accounting together with matching principle. They both determine the accounting period, in which revenues and expenses are recognized. According to the principle, revenues are recognized when they are (1) realized or realizable, and are (2) earned (usually when goods are transferred or services rendered), no matter when cash is received.

a. Tail risk
b. Regulation FD
c. Commodity Pool Operator
d. Revenue recognition

24. _____ is the portion of income that is the subject of taxation according to the laws that determine what is income and the taxation rate for that income. Generally, _____ refers to an individual's (or corporation's) gross income, adjusted for various deductions allowable by statute. The main questions put by most individuals in any jurisdiction are 'what makes up my _____' and what tax rates should be applied such that I can work out my tax liability to the state.

a. Taxable income
b. 7-Eleven
c. 4-4-5 Calendar
d. 529 plan

25. _____ is the provision of resources (such as granting a loan) by one party to another party where that second party does not reimburse the first party immediately, thereby generating a debt, and instead arranges either to repay or return those resources (or material(s) of equal value) at a later date. The first party is called a creditor, also known as a lender, while the second party is called a debtor, also known as a borrower.

Movements of financial capital are normally dependent on either _____ or equity transfers.

a. Comparable
b. Warrant
c. Clearing house
d. Credit

26. The term _____ describes two different concepts:

- The first is a recognition of partial payment already made towards taxes due.
- The second is a state benefit paid to workers through the tax system, which has the effect of increasing (rather than reducing) net income.

Within the Australian, Canadian, United Kingdom, and United States tax systems, a _____ is a recognition of partial payment already made towards taxes due. A similar concept exists (fr:Avoir fiscal) in the French tax system. This situation arises, for example, when standard rate tax has been deducted at source , but the tax-payer is subject to further taxation at a higher rate. It also applies in dividend imputation systems.

a. 7-Eleven
b. 529 plan
c. 4-4-5 Calendar
d. Tax credit

27. A _____ is a payment made by a corporation to its shareholder members. When a corporation earns a profit or surplus, that money can be put to two uses: it can either be re-invested in the business (called retained earnings), or it can be paid to the shareholders as a _____. Many corporations retain a portion of their earnings and pay the remainder as a _____.

a. Special dividend
b. Dividend yield
c. Dividend puzzle
d. Dividend

28. _____ is a corporate tax system in which some or all of the tax paid by a company may be attributed (or 'imputed') to the shareholders by way of a tax credit to reduce the income tax payable on a distribution. It reduces or eliminates the tax disadvantages of operating a business in a country.

Australia and New Zealand have imputation systems.

Chapter 21. Cross-Border Valuation

a. Special dividend
b. Dividend reinvestment plan
c. Dividend yield
d. Dividend imputation

29. _____ are formal records of a business' financial activities.

_____ provide an overview of a business' financial condition in both short and long term. There are four basic _____:

1. **Balance sheet**: also referred to as statement of financial position or condition, reports on a company's assets, liabilities, and net equity as of a given point in time.
2. **Income statement**: also referred to as Profit and Loss statement (or a 'P'L'), reports on a company's income, expenses, and profits over a period of time.
3. **Statement of retained earnings**: explains the changes in a company's retained earnings over the reporting period.
4. **Statement of cash flows**: reports on a company's cash flow activities, particularly its operating, investing and financing activities.

a. Statement of retained earnings
b. Statement on Auditing Standards No. 70: Service Organizations
c. Financial statements
d. Notes to the Financial Statements

30. The term _____ is used to describe a nation's social, or business activity in the process of rapid industrialization. _____ are generally less-wealthy than the developed world, and are wealthier (or the wealthiest of) the developing world. According to The Economist many people find the term dated, but a new term has yet to gain much traction.
a. Emerging markets
b. A Random Walk Down Wall Street
c. ABN Amro
d. AAB

31. In economics, _____ is a rise in the general level of prices of goods and services in an economy over a period of time. The term '_____' once referred to increases in the money supply (monetary _____); however, economic debates about the relationship between money supply and price levels have led to its primary use today in describing price _____. _____ can also be described as a decline in the real value of money--a loss of purchasing power in the medium of exchange which is also the monetary unit of account.
a. Inflation
b. ABN Amro
c. AAB
d. A Random Walk Down Wall Street

32. _____ is the balance of the amounts of cash being received and paid by a business during a defined period of time, sometimes tied to a specific project. Measurement of _____ can be used

- to evaluate the state or performance of a business or project.
- to determine problems with liquidity. Being profitable does not necessarily mean being liquid. A company can fail because of a shortage of cash, even while profitable.
- to generate project rate of returns. The time of _____s into and out of projects are used as inputs to financial models such as internal rate of return, and net present value.
- to examine income or growth of a business when it is believed that accrual accounting concepts do not represent economic realities. Alternately, _____ can be used to 'validate' the net income generated by accrual accounting.

_____ as a generic term may be used differently depending on context, and certain _____ definitions may be adapted by analysts and users for their own uses. Common terms include operating _____ and free _____.

_____s can be classified into:

1. Operational _____s: Cash received or expended as a result of the company's core business activities.
2. Investment _____s: Cash received or expended through capital expenditure, investments or acquisitions.
3. Financing _____s: Cash received or expended as a result of financial activities, such as interests and dividends.

All three together - the net _____ - are necessary to reconcile the beginning cash balance to the ending cash balance. Loan draw downs or equity injections, that is just shifting of capital but no expenditure as such, are not considered in the net _____.

a. Corporate finance
b. Real option
c. Shareholder value
d. Cash flow

33. The _____ is the rate that a company is expected to pay to finance its assets. WACC is the minimum return that a company must earn on existing asset base to satisfy its creditors, owners, and other providers of capital.

Companies raise money from a number of sources: common equity, preferred equity, straight debt, convertible debt, exchangeable debt, warrants, options, pension liabilities, executive stock options, governmental subsidies, and so on.

a. 4-4-5 Calendar
b. Cost of capital
c. Capital intensity
d. Weighted average cost of capital

34. In economics, business, and accounting, a _____ is the value of money that has been used up to produce something, and hence is not available for use anymore. In business, the _____ may be one of acquisition, in which case the amount of money expended to acquire it is counted as _____. In this case, money is the input that is gone in order to acquire the thing.

a. Fixed costs
b. Sliding scale fees
c. Marginal cost
d. Cost

35. The _____ is an expected return that the provider of capital plans to earn on their investment.

Capital (money) used for funding a business should earn returns for the capital providers who risk their capital. For an investment to be worthwhile, the expected return on capital must be greater than the _____.

a. Capital intensity
b. Weighted average cost of capital
c. 4-4-5 Calendar
d. Cost of capital

Chapter 21. Cross-Border Valuation

36. _____ is a fee paid on borrowed assets. It is the price paid for the use of borrowed money, or, money earned by deposited funds. Assets that are sometimes lent with _____ include money, shares, consumer goods through hire purchase, major assets such as aircraft, and even entire factories in finance lease arrangements.

a. A Random Walk Down Wall Street
b. Insolvency
c. Interest
d. AAB

37. An _____ is the price a borrower pays for the use of money they do not own, and the return a lender receives for deferring the use of funds, by lending it to the borrower. _____s are normally expressed as a percentage rate over the period of one year.

_____s targets are also a vital tool of monetary policy and are used to control variables like investment, inflation, and unemployment.

a. Interest rate
b. A Random Walk Down Wall Street
c. AAB
d. ABN Amro

38. Procter is a surname, and may also refer to:

- Bryan Waller Procter (pseud. Barry Cornwall), English poet
- Goodwin Procter, American law firm
- _____, consumer products multinational

a. Clearing house
b. Procter ' Gamble
c. Valuation
d. Bucket shop

39. A _____ is a portfolio consisting of a weighted sum of every asset in the market, with weights in the proportions that they exist in the market (with the necessary assumption that these assets are infinitely divisible.)

Neha Tyagi's critique (1977) states that this is only a theoretical concept, as to create a _____ for investment purposes in practice would necessarily include every single possible available asset, including real estate, precious metals, stamp collections, jewelry, and anything with any worth, as the theoretical market being referred to would be the world market. As a result, proxies for the market are used in practice by investors.

a. Central Securities Depository
b. Market portfolio
c. Market price
d. Delta neutral

Chapter 21. Cross-Border Valuation

40. _____ is a form of risk that arises from the change in price of one currency against another. Whenever investors or companies have assets or business operations across national borders, they face _____ if their positions are not hedged.

- Transaction risk is the risk that exchange rates will change unfavourably over time. It can be hedged against using forward currency contracts;
- Translation risk is an accounting risk, proportional to the amount of assets held in foreign currencies. Changes in the exchange rate over time will render a report inaccurate, and so assets are usually balanced by borrowings in that currency.

The exchange risk associated with a foreign denominated instrument is a key element in foreign investment. This risk flows from differential monetary policy and growth in real productivity, which results in differential inflation rates.

a. Credit risk
c. Market risk
b. Currency risk
d. Tracking error

41. _____ most frequently refers to the standard deviation of the continuously compounded returns of a financial instrument with a specific time horizon. It is often used to quantify the risk of the instrument over that time period. _____ is typically expressed in annualized terms, and it may either be an absolute number ($5) or a fraction of the mean (5%).

a. Seasoned equity offering
c. Volatility
b. Portfolio insurance
d. Currency swap

Chapter 22. Valuation in Emerging Markets

1. The term _____ is used to describe a nation's social, or business activity in the process of rapid industrialization. _____ are generally less-wealthy than the developed world, and are wealthier (or the wealthiest of) the developing world. According to The Economist many people find the term dated, but a new term has yet to gain much traction.
   a. A Random Walk Down Wall Street
   b. AAB
   c. ABN Amro
   d. Emerging markets

2. In economics, _____ is a rise in the general level of prices of goods and services in an economy over a period of time. The term '_____' once referred to increases in the money supply (monetary _____); however, economic debates about the relationship between money supply and price levels have led to its primary use today in describing price _____. _____ can also be described as a decline in the real value of money--a loss of purchasing power in the medium of exchange which is also the monetary unit of account.
   a. A Random Walk Down Wall Street
   b. AAB
   c. ABN Amro
   d. Inflation

3. _____ is a fee paid on borrowed assets. It is the price paid for the use of borrowed money , or, money earned by deposited funds . Assets that are sometimes lent with _____ include money, shares, consumer goods through hire purchase, major assets such as aircraft, and even entire factories in finance lease arrangements.
   a. A Random Walk Down Wall Street
   b. AAB
   c. Insolvency
   d. Interest

4. An _____ is the price a borrower pays for the use of money they do not own, and the return a lender receives for deferring the use of funds, by lending it to the borrower. _____s are normally expressed as a percentage rate over the period of one year.

   _____s targets are also a vital tool of monetary policy and are used to control variables like investment, inflation, and unemployment.

   a. Interest rate
   b. ABN Amro
   c. A Random Walk Down Wall Street
   d. AAB

5. The _____ is the rate that a company is expected to pay to finance its assets. WACC is the minimum return that a company must earn on existing asset base to satisfy its creditors, owners, and other providers of capital.

   Companies raise money from a number of sources: common equity, preferred equity, straight debt, convertible debt, exchangeable debt, warrants, options, pension liabilities, executive stock options, governmental subsidies, and so on.

   a. 4-4-5 Calendar
   b. Weighted average cost of capital
   c. Cost of capital
   d. Capital intensity

6. In finance, the _____ between two currencies specifies how much one currency is worth in terms of the other. For example an _____ of 102 Japanese yen to the United States dollar means that JPY 102 is worth the same as USD 1. The foreign exchange market is one of the largest markets in the world.
   a. ABN Amro
   b. AAB
   c. A Random Walk Down Wall Street
   d. Exchange rate

7. In financial accounting, a _____ or statement of financial position is a summary of a person's or organization's balances. Assets, liabilities and ownership equity are listed as of a specific date, such as the end of its financial year. A _____ is often described as a snapshot of a company's financial condition.

a. Statement on Auditing Standards No. 70: Service Organizations
b. Financial statements
c. Balance sheet
d. Statement of retained earnings

8. _____ are formal records of a business' financial activities.

_____ provide an overview of a business' financial condition in both short and long term. There are four basic _____:

1. **Balance sheet**: also referred to as statement of financial position or condition, reports on a company's assets, liabilities, and net equity as of a given point in time.
2. **Income statement**: also referred to as Profit and Loss statement (or a 'P'L'), reports on a company's income, expenses, and profits over a period of time.
3. **Statement of retained earnings**: explains the changes in a company's retained earnings over the reporting period.
4. **Statement of cash flows**: reports on a company's cash flow activities, particularly its operating, investing and financing activities.

a. Statement on Auditing Standards No. 70: Service Organizations
b. Financial statements
c. Statement of retained earnings
d. Notes to the Financial Statements

9. _____, refers to consumption opportunity gained by an entity within a specified time frame, which is generally expressed in monetary terms. However, for households and individuals, '_____ is the sum of all the wages, salaries, profits, interests payments, rents and other forms of earnings received... in a given period of time.' For firms, _____ generally refers to net-profit: what remains of revenue after expenses have been subtracted.

a. Accrual
b. Annual report
c. OIBDA
d. Income

10. An _____ is a financial statement for companies that indicates how Revenue is transformed into net income The purpose of the _____ is to show managers and investors whether the company made or lost money during the period being reported.

The important thing to remember about an _____ is that it represents a period of time.

a. ABN Amro
b. A Random Walk Down Wall Street
c. AAB
d. Income statement

Chapter 22. Valuation in Emerging Markets

11. _____ is the balance of the amounts of cash being received and paid by a business during a defined period of time, sometimes tied to a specific project. Measurement of _____ can be used

- to evaluate the state or performance of a business or project.
- to determine problems with liquidity. Being profitable does not necessarily mean being liquid. A company can fail because of a shortage of cash, even while profitable.
- to generate project rate of returns. The time of _____s into and out of projects are used as inputs to financial models such as internal rate of return, and net present value.
- to examine income or growth of a business when it is believed that accrual accounting concepts do not represent economic realities. Alternately, _____ can be used to 'validate' the net income generated by accrual accounting.

_____ as a generic term may be used differently depending on context, and certain _____ definitions may be adapted by analysts and users for their own uses. Common terms include operating _____ and free _____.

_____s can be classified into:

1. Operational _____s: Cash received or expended as a result of the company's core business activities.
2. Investment _____s: Cash received or expended through capital expenditure, investments or acquisitions.
3. Financing _____s: Cash received or expended as a result of financial activities, such as interests and dividends.

All three together - the net _____ - are necessary to reconcile the beginning cash balance to the ending cash balance. Loan draw downs or equity injections, that is just shifting of capital but no expenditure as such, are not considered in the net _____.

a. Cash flow
b. Real option
c. Shareholder value
d. Corporate finance

12. In corporate finance, _____ is a cash flow available for distribution among all the security holders of a company. They include equity holders, debt holders, preferred stock holders, convertible security holders, and so on.

Note that the first three lines above are calculated for you on the standard Statement of Cash Flows.

a. Free cash flow
b. Safety stock
c. Forfaiting
d. Funding

13. _____ is a finance term describing a firm's non-Equity cash flows. Theoretically, adding the discounted _____ to the discounted Flows to equity (also known as Equity Cash Flows) will give the firm's Enterprise Value. The Enterprise value is the valuation obtained by calculating the Discounted Cash Flow.

a. Foreign exchange hedge
b. Par value
c. Debt cash flow
d. Consignment stock

Chapter 22. Valuation in Emerging Markets

14. In finance, _____ is the process of estimating the potential market value of a financial asset or liability. they can be done on assets (for example, investments in marketable securities such as stocks, options, business enterprises, or intangible assets such as patents and trademarks) or on liabilities (e.g., Bonds issued by a company.) _____s are required in many contexts including investment analysis, capital budgeting, merger and acquisition transactions, financial reporting, taxable events to determine the proper tax liability, and in litigation.
    a. Procter ' Gamble
    b. Share
    c. Valuation
    d. Margin

15. _____ refers to the likelihood that changes in the business environment adversely affect operating profits or the value of assets in a specific country. For example, financial factors such as currency controls, devaluation or regulatory changes, or stability factors such as mass riots, civil war and other potential events contribute to companies' operational risks. This term is also sometimes referred to as political risk, however _____ is a more general term, which generally only refers to risks affecting all companies operating within a particular country.
    a. Capital asset
    b. Country risk
    c. Single-index model
    d. Solvency

16.

In finance, the _____ can be the expected rate of return above the risk-free interest rate. When measuring risk, a common sense approach is to compare the risk-free return on T-bills and the very risky return on other investments. The difference between these two returns can be interpreted as a measure of the excess return on the average risky asset. This excess return is known as the _____.

    a. Risk aversion
    b. Risk modeling
    c. Risk adjusted return on capital
    d. Risk premium

17. In economics, business, and accounting, a _____ is the value of money that has been used up to produce something, and hence is not available for use anymore. In business, the _____ may be one of acquisition, in which case the amount of money expended to acquire it is counted as _____. In this case, money is the input that is gone in order to acquire the thing.
    a. Fixed costs
    b. Cost
    c. Sliding scale fees
    d. Marginal cost

18. The _____ is an expected return that the provider of capital plans to earn on their investment.

Capital (money) used for funding a business should earn returns for the capital providers who risk their capital. For an investment to be worthwhile, the expected return on capital must be greater than the _____.

    a. 4-4-5 Calendar
    b. Cost of capital
    c. Capital intensity
    d. Weighted average cost of capital

Chapter 22. Valuation in Emerging Markets

19. The term _____ has three unrelated technical definitions, and is also used in a variety of non-technical ways.

   - In financial economics, it refers to any asset used to make money, as opposed to assets used for personal enjoyment or consumption. This is an important distinction because two people can disagree sharply about the value of personal assets, one person might think a sports car is more valuable than a pickup truck, another person might have the opposite taste. But if an asset is held for the purpose of making money, taste has nothing to do with it, only differences of opinion about how much money the asset will produce. With the further assumption that people agree on the probability distribution of future cash flows, it is possible to have an objective _____ pricing model. Even without the assumption of agreement, it is possible to set rational limits on _____ value.
   - In governmental accounting, it is defined as any asset used in operations with an initial useful life extending beyond one reporting period. Generally, government managers have a 'stewardship' duty to maintain _____s under their control. See International Public Sector Accounting Standards for details.
   - In US tax accounting, it is defined as any property other than a list of exceptions. The main exceptions are anything held for sale, and any real estate or depreciable property used in business. Almost everything you own and use for personal purposes, pleasure or investment is a _____. If something is a _____ for tax purposes, gains or losses on sale or disposition are capital gains or capital losses. For individuals, however, capital losses on property held for personal use are generally not deductible. See the IRS publication Tax Facts about Capital Gains and Losses for details.

A well-known financial accounting textbook advises that the term be avoided except in tax accounting because it is used in so many different senses, not all of them well-defined. For example it is often used as a synonym for fixed assets or for investments in securities.

A common non-technical usage occurs when people ask that employees or the environment or something else be treated as a _____.

   a. Capital asset
   c. Political risk
   b. Solvency
   d. Settlement date

20. In finance, the _____ is used to determine a theoretically appropriate required rate of return of an asset, if that asset is to be added to an already well-diversified portfolio, given that asset's non-diversifiable risk. The model takes into account the asset's sensitivity to non-diversifiable risk (also known as systemic risk or market risk), often represented by the quantity beta (β) in the financial industry, as well as the expected return of the market and the expected return of a theoretical risk-free asset.

The model was introduced by Jack Treynor (1961, 1962), William Sharpe (1964), John Lintner (1965a,b) and Jan Mossin (1966) independently, building on the earlier work of Harry Markowitz on diversification and modern portfolio theory.

   a. Hull-White model
   c. Cox-Ingersoll-Ross model
   b. Capital asset pricing model
   d. Random walk hypothesis

21. In business and accounting, _____s are everything of value that is owned by a person or company. The balance sheet of a firm records the monetary value of the _____s owned by the firm. The two major _____ classes are tangible _____s and intangible _____s.

Chapter 22. Valuation in Emerging Markets

a. Income
b. Accounts payable
c. Asset
d. EBITDA

22. In finance, the _____ is the minimum rate of return a firm must offer shareholders to compensate for waiting for their returns, and for bearing some risk.

The _____ capital for a particular company is the rate of return on investment that is required by the company's ordinary shareholders. The return consists both of dividend and capital gains, e.g. increases in the share price.

a. Round-tripping
b. Net pay
c. Residual value
d. Cost of equity

23. _____ is that which is owed; usually referencing assets owed, but the term can cover other obligations. In the case of assets, _____ is a means of using future purchasing power in the present before a summation has been earned. Some companies and corporations use _____ as a part of their overall corporate finance strategy.

a. Cross-collateralization
b. Partial Payment
c. Credit cycle
d. Debt

24. _____ is the risk that the value of an investment will decrease due to moves in market factors. The five standard _____ factors are:

- Equity risk, the risk that stock prices will change.
- Interest rate risk, the risk that interest rates will change.
- Currency risk, the risk that foreign exchange rates will change.
- Commodity risk, the risk that commodity prices (e.g. grains, metals) will change.

As with other forms of risk, _____ may be measured in a number of ways. Traditionally, this is done using a Value at Risk methodology. Value at risk is well established as a risk management technique, but it contains a number of limiting assumptions that constrain its accuracy.

a. Currency risk
b. Transaction risk
c. Tracking error
d. Market risk

25. _____ is a business valuation method. _____ is the net present value of a project if financed solely by ownership equity plus the present value of all the benefits of financing. Usually, the main benefit is a tax shield resulted from tax deductibility of interest payments. Another one can be a subsidized borrowing.

a. A Random Walk Down Wall Street
b. AAB
c. ABN Amro
d. Adjusted present value

26. _____ is the value on a given date of a future payment or series of future payments, discounted to reflect the time value of money and other factors such as investment risk. _____ calculations are widely used in business and economics to provide a means to compare cash flows at different times on a meaningful 'like to like' basis.

The most commonly applied model of the time value of money is compound interest.

a. Net present value
b. Present value of benefits
c. Negative gearing
d. Present value

Chapter 23. Valuing High-Growth Companies

1. _____ is a finance term describing a firm's non-Equity cash flows. Theoretically, adding the discounted _____ to the discounted Flows to equity (also known as Equity Cash Flows) will give the firm's Enterprise Value. The Enterprise value is the valuation obtained by calculating the Discounted Cash Flow.
   - a. Par value
   - b. Foreign exchange hedge
   - c. Consignment stock
   - d. Debt cash flow

2. _____ is the balance of the amounts of cash being received and paid by a business during a defined period of time, sometimes tied to a specific project. Measurement of _____ can be used

   - to evaluate the state or performance of a business or project.
   - to determine problems with liquidity. Being profitable does not necessarily mean being liquid. A company can fail because of a shortage of cash, even while profitable.
   - to generate project rate of returns. The time of _____s into and out of projects are used as inputs to financial models such as internal rate of return, and net present value.
   - to examine income or growth of a business when it is believed that accrual accounting concepts do not represent economic realities. Alternately, _____ can be used to 'validate' the net income generated by accrual accounting.

   _____ as a generic term may be used differently depending on context, and certain _____ definitions may be adapted by analysts and users for their own uses. Common terms include operating _____ and free _____.

   _____s can be classified into:

   1. Operational _____s: Cash received or expended as a result of the company's core business activities.
   2. Investment _____s: Cash received or expended through capital expenditure, investments or acquisitions.
   3. Financing _____s: Cash received or expended as a result of financial activities, such as interests and dividends.

   All three together - the net _____ - are necessary to reconcile the beginning cash balance to the ending cash balance. Loan draw downs or equity injections, that is just shifting of capital but no expenditure as such, are not considered in the net _____.

   - a. Corporate finance
   - b. Real option
   - c. Shareholder value
   - d. Cash flow

3. In finance, _____ is the process of estimating the potential market value of a financial asset or liability. they can be done on assets (for example, investments in marketable securities such as stocks, options, business enterprises, or intangible assets such as patents and trademarks) or on liabilities (e.g., Bonds issued by a company.) _____s are required in many contexts including investment analysis, capital budgeting, merger and acquisition transactions, financial reporting, taxable events to determine the proper tax liability, and in litigation.
   - a. Margin
   - b. Share
   - c. Valuation
   - d. Procter ' Gamble

Chapter 23. Valuing High-Growth Companies

4. In business, _____ is income that a company receives from its normal business activities, usually from the sale of goods and services to customers. Some companies also receive _____ from interest, dividends or royalties paid to them by other companies. _____ may refer to business income in general, or it may refer to the amount, in a monetary unit, received during a period of time, as in 'Last year, Company X had _____ of $32 million.'

In many countries, including the UK, _____ is referred to as turnover.

 a. Furniture, Fixtures and Equipment
 b. Bottom line
 c. Matching principle
 d. Revenue

5. A _____ is the price of a single share of a no. of saleable stocks of the company. Once the stock is purchased, the owner becomes a shareholder of the company that issued the share.
 a. Whisper numbers
 b. Trading curb
 c. Stock split
 d. Share price

6. _____ most frequently refers to the standard deviation of the continuously compounded returns of a financial instrument with a specific time horizon. It is often used to quantify the risk of the instrument over that time period. _____ is typically expressed in annualized terms, and it may either be an absolute number ($5) or a fraction of the mean (5%).
 a. Currency swap
 b. Seasoned equity offering
 c. Portfolio insurance
 d. Volatility

Chapter 24. Valuing Cyclical Companies

1. In business and finance, a _____ (also referred to as equity _____) of stock means a _____ of ownership in a corporation (company.) In the plural, stocks is often used as a synonym for _____s especially in the United States, but it is less commonly used that way outside of North America.

In the United Kingdom, South Africa, and Australia, stock can also refer to completely different financial instruments such as government bonds or, less commonly, to all kinds of marketable securities.

   a. Share
   b. Margin
   c. Procter ' Gamble
   d. Bucket shop

2. A _____ is the price of a single share of a no. of saleable stocks of the company. Once the stock is purchased, the owner becomes a shareholder of the company that issued the share.
   a. Whisper numbers
   b. Trading curb
   c. Stock split
   d. Share price

3. In finance, _____ is the process of estimating the potential market value of a financial asset or liability. they can be done on assets (for example, investments in marketable securities such as stocks, options, business enterprises, or intangible assets such as patents and trademarks) or on liabilities (e.g., Bonds issued by a company.) _____s are required in many contexts including investment analysis, capital budgeting, merger and acquisition transactions, financial reporting, taxable events to determine the proper tax liability, and in litigation.
   a. Share
   b. Margin
   c. Valuation
   d. Procter ' Gamble

4. A _____ is something for which there is demand, but which is supplied without qualitative differentiation across a market. It is a product that is the same no matter who produces it, such as petroleum, notebook paper, or milk. In other words, copper is copper.
   a. 4-4-5 Calendar
   b. Commodity
   c. 529 plan
   d. 7-Eleven

5. A _____ is an expenditure creating future benefits. A _____ is incurred when a business spends money either to buy fixed assets or to add to the value of an existing fixed asset with a useful life that extends beyond the taxable year. Capex are used by a company to acquire or upgrade physical assets such as equipment, property, or industrial buildings.
   a. Weighted average cost of capital
   b. 4-4-5 Calendar
   c. Cost of capital
   d. Capital expenditure

Chapter 25. Valuing Financial Institutions

1. _____ is the balance of the amounts of cash being received and paid by a business during a defined period of time, sometimes tied to a specific project. Measurement of _____ can be used

   - to evaluate the state or performance of a business or project.
   - to determine problems with liquidity. Being profitable does not necessarily mean being liquid. A company can fail because of a shortage of cash, even while profitable.
   - to generate project rate of returns. The time of _____s into and out of projects are used as inputs to financial models such as internal rate of return, and net present value.
   - to examine income or growth of a business when it is believed that accrual accounting concepts do not represent economic realities. Alternately, _____ can be used to 'validate' the net income generated by accrual accounting.

   _____ as a generic term may be used differently depending on context, and certain _____ definitions may be adapted by analysts and users for their own uses. Common terms include operating _____ and free _____.

   _____s can be classified into:

   1. Operational _____s: Cash received or expended as a result of the company's core business activities.
   2. Investment _____s: Cash received or expended through capital expenditure, investments or acquisitions.
   3. Financing _____s: Cash received or expended as a result of financial activities, such as interests and dividends.

   All three together - the net _____ - are necessary to reconcile the beginning cash balance to the ending cash balance. Loan draw downs or equity injections, that is just shifting of capital but no expenditure as such, are not considered in the net _____.

   a. Real option
   c. Corporate finance
   b. Shareholder value
   d. Cash flow

2. In finance, _____ is the process of estimating the potential market value of a financial asset or liability. they can be done on assets (for example, investments in marketable securities such as stocks, options, business enterprises, or intangible assets such as patents and trademarks) or on liabilities (e.g., Bonds issued by a company.) _____s are required in many contexts including investment analysis, capital budgeting, merger and acquisition transactions, financial reporting, taxable events to determine the proper tax liability, and in litigation.
   a. Share
   c. Margin
   b. Procter ' Gamble
   d. Valuation

3. Risk adjusted return on capital (_____) is a risk-based profitability measurement framework for analysing risk-adjusted financial performance and providing a consistent view of profitability across businesses. The concept was developed by Bankers Trust in the late 1970s. Note, however, that more and more Risk Adjusted Return on Risk Adjusted Capital (RARORAC) is used as a measure, whereby the risk adjustment of Capital is based on the capital adequacy guidelines as outlined by the Basel Committee, currently Basel II.
   a. Value at risk
   c. Discount factor
   b. RAROC
   d. Risk modeling

Chapter 25. Valuing Financial Institutions

4. In business and accounting, _____s are everything of value that is owned by a person or company. The balance sheet of a firm records the monetary value of the _____s owned by the firm. The two major _____ classes are tangible _____s and intangible _____s.
  a. Asset
  c. Income
  b. Accounts payable
  d. EBITDA

5. _____ is an accounting term used to reflect the portion of the book value of a business entity not directly attributable to its assets and liabilities; it normally arises only in case of an acquisition. It reflects the ability of the entity to make a higher profit than would be derived from selling the tangible assets. _____ is also known as an intangible asset.
  a. Net profit
  c. Goodwill
  b. Consolidation
  d. Cost of goods sold

6. _____ is the process of decreasing an amount over a period of time. The word comes from Middle English amortisen to kill, alienate in mortmain, from Anglo-French amorteser, alteration of amortir, from Vulgar Latin admortire to kill, from Latin ad- + mort-, mors death. Particular instances of the term include:

  - _____ (business), the allocation of a lump sum amount to different time periods, particularly for loans and other forms of finance, including related interest or other finance charges.
    - _____ schedule, a table detailing each periodic payment on a loan (typically a mortgage), as generated by an _____ calculator.
    - Negative _____, an _____ schedule where the loan amount actually increases through not paying the full interest
  - Amortized analysis, analyzing the execution cost of algorithms over a sequence of operations.
  - _____ of capital expenditures of certain assets under accounting rules, particularly intangible assets, in a manner analogous to depreciation.
  - _____ (tax law)

_____ is also used in the context of zoning regulations and describes the time in which a property owner has to relocate when the property's use constitutes a preexisting nonconforming use under zoning regulations.

  - Depreciation

  a. Amortization
  c. AT'T Inc.
  b. Intrinsic value
  d. Option

7. Pure _____ is the increase in wealth that an investor has from making an investment, taking into consideration all costs associated with that investment including the opportunity cost of capital.

A key difficulty in measuring profit is in defining costs. Pure economic monetary profits can be zero or negative even in competitive equilibrium when accounted monetized costs exceed monetized price.

  a. AAB
  c. Economic profit
  b. A Random Walk Down Wall Street
  d. Operating profit

Chapter 25. Valuing Financial Institutions

8. In corporate finance, _____ is a cash flow available for distribution among all the security holders of a company. They include equity holders, debt holders, preferred stock holders, convertible security holders, and so on.

Note that the first three lines above are calculated for you on the standard Statement of Cash Flows.

a. Free cash flow
c. Forfaiting
b. Safety stock
d. Funding

9. _____ is the difference between price and the costs of bringing to market whatever it is that is accounted as an enterprise (whether by harvest, extraction, manufacture, or purchase) in terms of the component costs of delivered goods and/or services and any operating or other expenses.

A key difficulty in measuring profit is in defining costs. Pure economic monetary profits can be zero or negative even in competitive equilibrium when accounted monetized costs exceed monetized price.

a. Economic profit
c. Accounting profit
b. A Random Walk Down Wall Street
d. AAB

10. _____, refers to consumption opportunity gained by an entity within a specified time frame, which is generally expressed in monetary terms. However, for households and individuals, '_____ is the sum of all the wages, salaries, profits, interests payments, rents and other forms of earnings received... in a given period of time.' For firms, _____ generally refers to net-profit: what remains of revenue after expenses have been subtracted.

a. Income
c. Annual report
b. OIBDA
d. Accrual

11. An _____ is a financial statement for companies that indicates how Revenue is transformed into net income The purpose of the _____ is to show managers and investors whether the company made or lost money during the period being reported.

The important thing to remember about an _____ is that it represents a period of time.

a. ABN Amro
c. A Random Walk Down Wall Street
b. Income statement
d. AAB

12. In finance, _____ refers to the way a corporation finances its assets through some combination of equity, debt, or hybrid securities. A firm's _____ is then the composition or 'structure' of its liabilities. For example, a firm that sells $20 billion in equity and $80 billion in debt is said to be 20% equity-financed and 80% debt-financed.

a. Rights issue
c. Market for corporate control
b. Capital structure
d. Book building

13. In financial accounting, a _____ or statement of financial position is a summary of a person's or organization's balances. Assets, liabilities and ownership equity are listed as of a specific date, such as the end of its financial year. A _____ is often described as a snapshot of a company's financial condition.

Chapter 25. Valuing Financial Institutions

a. Balance sheet

c. Financial statements

b. Statement of retained earnings

d. Statement on Auditing Standards No. 70: Service Organizations

14. _____ is the standard framework of guidelines for financial accounting used in the United States of America. It includes the standards, conventions, and rules accountants follow in recording and summarizing transactions, and in the preparation of financial statements. _____ are now issued by the Financial Accounting Standards Board (FASB).
  a. Depreciation
  c. Generally Accepted Accounting Principles
  b. Net income
  d. Revenue

15. The U.S. _____ is an independent agency of the United States government which holds primary responsibility for enforcing the federal securities laws and regulating the securities industry, the nation's stock and options exchanges, and other electronic securities markets. The SEC was created by section 4 of the SEC of 1934 (now codified as 15 U.S.C. Â§ 78d and commonly referred to as the 1934 Act.)
  a. 4-4-5 Calendar
  c. 7-Eleven
  b. Securities and Exchange Commission
  d. 529 plan

16. Two primary _____, cash and accrual basis, and their combination, called modified cash basis, are used in recognizing income (revenues) and expenses in bookkeeping in order to measure net income for a specified time interval (accounting period.) Both methods differ on such recognition leading to varying income recordings, which may be subject to error or - manipulation. Many financial scandals involved accounting manipulations.
  a. Accounting equation
  c. Asset
  b. Outstanding balance
  d. Accounting methods

17. The phrase _____ refers to the aspect of corporate strategy, corporate finance and management dealing with the buying, selling and combining of different companies that can aid, finance, or help a growing company in a given industry grow rapidly without having to create another business entity.

An acquisition, also known as a takeover, is the buying of one company (the 'target') by another. An acquisition may be friendly or hostile.

  a. 529 plan
  c. Mergers and acquisitions
  b. 7-Eleven
  d. 4-4-5 Calendar

18. In economics, business, and accounting, a _____ is the value of money that has been used up to produce something, and hence is not available for use anymore. In business, the _____ may be one of acquisition, in which case the amount of money expended to acquire it is counted as _____. In this case, money is the input that is gone in order to acquire the thing.
  a. Cost
  c. Sliding scale fees
  b. Marginal cost
  d. Fixed costs

19. _____, in accrual accounting, is any account where the asset or liability is not realized until a future date, e.g. annuities, charges, taxes, income, etc. The _____ item may be carried, dependent on type of deferral, as either an asset or liability.See also: accrual

_____ is also used in the university admissions process. It is the action by which a school rejects a student for early admission but still opts to review that student in the general admissions pool.

a. Revenue
b. Deferred
c. Net profit
d. Current asset

20. In financial accounting, the term _____ is most commonly used to describe any part of shareholders' equity, except for basic share capital. Sometimes, the term is used instead of the term provision; such a use, however, is inconsistent with the terminology suggested by International Accounting Standards Board. For more information about provisions, see provision (accounting.)
a. Treasury stock
b. Closing entries
c. FIFO and LIFO accounting
d. Reserve

21. The _____ is the rate that a company is expected to pay to finance its assets. WACC is the minimum return that a company must earn on existing asset base to satisfy its creditors, owners, and other providers of capital.

Companies raise money from a number of sources: common equity, preferred equity, straight debt, convertible debt, exchangeable debt, warrants, options, pension liabilities, executive stock options, governmental subsidies, and so on.

a. Cost of capital
b. Weighted average cost of capital
c. 4-4-5 Calendar
d. Capital intensity

22. The _____ is an expected return that the provider of capital plans to earn on their investment.

Capital (money) used for funding a business should earn returns for the capital providers who risk their capital. For an investment to be worthwhile, the expected return on capital must be greater than the _____.

a. Weighted average cost of capital
b. 4-4-5 Calendar
c. Capital intensity
d. Cost of capital

23. In finance, the _____ approach describes a method of valuing a project, company, or asset using the concepts of the time value of money. All future cash flows are estimated and discounted to give their present values. The discount rate used is generally the appropriate cost of capital and may incorporate judgments of the uncertainty (riskiness) of the future cash flows.
a. Net present value
b. Future-oriented
c. Present value of benefits
d. Discounted cash flow

24. _____ is a business valuation method. _____ is the net present value of a project if financed solely by ownership equity plus the present value of all the benefits of financing. Usually, the main benefit is a tax shield resulted from tax deductibility of interest payments. Another one can be a subsidized borrowing.
a. A Random Walk Down Wall Street
b. ABN Amro
c. Adjusted present value
d. AAB

Chapter 25. Valuing Financial Institutions

25. _____ is a finance term describing a firm's non-Equity cash flows. Theoretically, adding the discounted _____ to the discounted Flows to equity (also known as Equity Cash Flows) will give the firm's Enterprise Value. The Enterprise value is the valuation obtained by calculating the Discounted Cash Flow.

   a. Foreign exchange hedge   b. Debt cash flow
   c. Par value   d. Consignment stock

26. _____ is the value on a given date of a future payment or series of future payments, discounted to reflect the time value of money and other factors such as investment risk. _____ calculations are widely used in business and economics to provide a means to compare cash flows at different times on a meaningful 'like to like' basis.

The most commonly applied model of the time value of money is compound interest.

   a. Net present value   b. Negative gearing
   c. Present value of benefits   d. Present value

27. In finance, the _____ is the minimum rate of return a firm must offer shareholders to compensate for waiting for their returns, and for bearing some risk.

The _____ capital for a particular company is the rate of return on investment that is required by the company's ordinary shareholders. The return consists both of dividend and capital gains, e.g. increases in the share price.

   a. Residual value   b. Cost of equity
   c. Round-tripping   d. Net pay

28. _____ is the provision of resources (such as granting a loan) by one party to another party where that second party does not reimburse the first party immediately, thereby generating a debt, and instead arranges either to repay or return those resources (or material(s) of equal value) at a later date. The first party is called a creditor, also known as a lender, while the second party is called a debtor, also known as a borrower.

Movements of financial capital are normally dependent on either _____ or equity transfers.

   a. Clearing house   b. Warrant
   c. Comparable   d. Credit

29. A _____ assesses the credit worthiness of an individual, corporation, or even a country. _____s are calculated from financial history and current assets and liabilities. Typically, a _____ tells a lender or investor the probability of the subject being able to pay back a loan.

   a. Credit rating   b. Credit cycle
   c. Debenture   d. Credit report monitoring

30. The _____ of a stock is a measure of the price paid for a share relative to the annual income or profit earned by the firm per share. It is a financial ratio used for valuation: a higher _____ means that investors are paying more for each unit of income, so the stock is more expensive compared to one with lower _____.

The _____ has units of years, which can be interpreted as 'number of years of earnings to pay back purchase price'.

a. Return of capital
b. Quick ratio
c. Sustainable growth rate
d. P/E ratio

ANSWER KEY

Chapter 1
1. c   2. a   3. b   4. d   5. d   6. d   7. d   8. a   9. d   10. c
11. b   12. a   13. b

Chapter 2
1. d   2. d   3. d   4. a   5. b   6. d

Chapter 3
1. c   2. d   3. d   4. a   5. d   6. a   7. b   8. a   9. d   10. d
11. d   12. d   13. c   14. b

Chapter 4
1. d   2. d   3. a   4. a   5. d   6. d   7. a   8. c   9. a   10. a
11. d   12. c   13. d   14. c   15. b   16. b   17. b   18. a   19. d   20. b
21. d

Chapter 5
1. c   2. b   3. a   4. d   5. b   6. c   7. a   8. d   9. d   10. d
11. c   12. d   13. d   14. c   15. b   16. d   17. b   18. b   19. b   20. c
21. b   22. a   23. c   24. a   25. d   26. b   27. b   28. c   29. d   30. d
31. d   32. a   33. d   34. c   35. d   36. c   37. d   38. c   39. c

Chapter 6
1. d   2. b   3. d   4. d   5. d   6. a   7. d   8. b

Chapter 7
1. c   2. d   3. d   4. d   5. d   6. a   7. a   8. c   9. d   10. a
11. d   12. b   13. c   14. d   15. d   16. d   17. d   18. a   19. d   20. d
21. d   22. d   23. d   24. d   25. a   26. c   27. c   28. d   29. d   30. b
31. d   32. b   33. d   34. a   35. d   36. a   37. d   38. a   39. c   40. b
41. c   42. c   43. a   44. b   45. d   46. d   47. b   48. a   49. d   50. d
51. d   52. d   53. d   54. d   55. d   56. d   57. d   58. d   59. d   60. a
61. d   62. b   63. d   64. d

Chapter 8
1. b   2. c   3. a   4. d   5. a   6. d   7. a   8. c   9. c   10. d
11. d   12. c   13. d   14. d   15. b   16. b   17. d   18. a   19. a   20. a
21. a   22. d   23. d   24. d   25. d   26. d   27. c   28. d   29. d   30. d
31. d   32. d   33. a   34. a

Chapter 9
1. b   2. a   3. d   4. a   5. c   6. b   7. b   8. a   9. c   10. c
11. d   12. d   13. b

Chapter 10
1. a	2. c	3. d	4. a	5. d	6. c	7. d	8. c	9. d	10. b
11. a	12. d	13. c	14. c	15. d	16. a	17. d	18. d	19. c	20. a
21. a	22. d	23. b	24. d	25. d	26. d	27. d	28. b	29. d	30. d
31. a	32. d								

Chapter 11
1. d	2. d	3. a	4. b	5. b	6. b	7. c	8. b	9. d	10. b
11. b	12. b	13. c	14. b	15. c	16. d	17. b	18. a	19. d	20. b
21. b	22. b	23. c	24. c	25. b	26. d				

Chapter 12
1. a	2. d	3. a	4. d	5. a	6. d	7. d	8. a	9. a	10. c

Chapter 13
1. d	2. d	3. d	4. a	5. a	6. d	7. b	8. d	9. d	10. d

Chapter 14
1. c	2. d	3. a	4. d	5. c	6. b

Chapter 15
1. b	2. c	3. b	4. b	5. d	6. b	7. d	8. d	9. c	10. d
11. a	12. d	13. d							

Chapter 16
1. d	2. d	3. d	4. a	5. b

Chapter 17
1. b	2. d	3. d	4. b	5. a	6. a	7. d	8. d	9. d	10. a
11. c	12. d	13. b	14. d	15. d	16. a	17. d	18. d	19. a	20. d
21. c	22. a	23. d	24. c	25. d	26. c	27. a	28. d	29. c	30. d
31. b	32. d								

Chapter 18
1. d	2. d	3. d	4. b	5. d	6. a	7. d	8. d	9. b	10. d
11. d	12. d								

Chapter 19
1. d	2. d	3. c	4. c	5. b	6. d	7. d	8. a	9. d	10. d

Chapter 20
1. c	2. d	3. d	4. d	5. b	6. b	7. c	8. d	9. c	10. d
11. b	12. d								

ANSWER KEY

Chapter 21
1. b   2. c   3. d   4. d   5. d   6. a   7. d   8. d   9. a   10. b
11. d   12. d   13. a   14. d   15. d   16. d   17. d   18. a   19. c   20. c
21. c   22. d   23. d   24. a   25. d   26. d   27. d   28. d   29. c   30. a
31. a   32. d   33. d   34. d   35. d   36. c   37. a   38. b   39. b   40. b
41. c

Chapter 22
1. d   2. d   3. d   4. a   5. b   6. d   7. c   8. b   9. d   10. d
11. a   12. a   13. c   14. c   15. b   16. d   17. b   18. b   19. a   20. b
21. c   22. d   23. d   24. d   25. d   26. d

Chapter 23
1. d   2. d   3. c   4. d   5. d   6. d

Chapter 24
1. a   2. d   3. c   4. b   5. d

Chapter 25
1. d   2. d   3. b   4. a   5. c   6. a   7. c   8. a   9. c   10. a
11. b   12. b   13. a   14. c   15. b   16. d   17. c   18. a   19. b   20. d
21. b   22. d   23. d   24. c   25. b   26. d   27. b   28. d   29. a   30. d